VIENNA
Architecture and Art

C000126046

Contents

Beginnings and Middle Ages

History

Its location on the Danube, the only major European river connecting the west and the east, as well as on the pre-Roman north-south route of the Amber Road, destined the Viennese basin to become a key trading centre. By the Neolithic period (5500–2300 BCE) at the latest settlements already existed here in numerous locations. These grew in density in the late Bronze Age (approximately 1000 BCE), with larger open settlements including burial grounds in the south and an extensive hilltop settlement on the Leopoldsberg. This mountain, sloping to the Danube, remained a favourite site for settlements in subsequent periods. Particularly the Celts, who arrived in the area around Vienna from the west in the 4th century BCE, chose this location. About 150 BCE the largest hilltop site in the region was located here, the ledges in the terrain on the eastern and southern faces still recognizable today are remains of the settlement's walls. The Leopoldsberg retained its importance as a military fortification in later periods (a fort is documented there for the 13th century) and played a key role as the si-

p. 2: St Mary on the Bank, view of west façade from Gasse Am-Gestade, 1394–1414 (cf. pp. 24–26)

Leopoldsberg (19th District), site of the most important Celtic settlement (2 BCE) with Baroque Leopold church

te of Marco d'Aviano's mass before the battle to relieve Vienna in 1683. Since then the miraculous image of "Maria Hilfe der Christen" [St Mary, Succour to Christians], also known as "Maria Türkenhilf" [St Mary, Aid against the Turks] has been venerated in the Baroque church of St Leopold.

During the Roman period the legionnaire camp of Vindobona was established on the location of present-day Vienna. Under Emperor Augustus the former Celtic kingdom of Noricum was absorbed in 15 CE into the Roman province of Pannonia, with the Danube forming the border with the Germanic tribes located to the north. The most important military base on the border was initially Carnuntum, where the 15th legion was stationed, reinforced by the outpost at Vindobona. This outpost was probably located in the area between the Freyung square and Schottenkloster [Scottish Monastery], i.e. in the area of medieval Vienna. Under Emperor Domitian a larger permanent garrison (circa 455 x 500m) was established at the end of the first century CE for the 13th legion, further eastwards on a high plateau east of the Tiefen Graben und north of the Naglergasse. An extensive and separate civilian settlement grew up approximately 2 km southeast of the camp, stretching from the Botanical Garden to Aspang Train Station (3d district).

The legion's garrison Vindobona was completely destroyed in 169, when the Germanic tribes of the Marcomanni and Quadi from the north banks of the Danube penetrated deep into Italy. Claudi-

us Pompeianus, son-in-law of Emperor Marcus Aurelius, was able to reconquer the area with a direct counterattack. Vindobona was rebuilt and the Danube border was fortified. A period of relative prosperity followed, during which the civilian settlement received Roman civil rights and wine was cultivated. In the late 3d century however the Danube border became increasingly insecure, due to the constant influx of eastern peoples, and after the death of Emperor Valentinian in 375 at the latest the Romans lost control of Pannonia to various Germanic tribes. Around the year 400 the legion's garrison, the civilian town and its suburbs fell prey to an attack that signalled the end of Roman civilisation. The civilian town was ultimately abandoned; small remnants of the population, as well as the wandering peoples of the Lombards and Avars, settled during the next centuries in the ruins of the castrum, whose walls offered protection for many centuries.

Although the area around Vienna was already integrated into Charlemagne's Frankish kingdom in the late 8th century, the city itself was only able to grow slowly. The Carolingian period was marked by intensive missionary activity, carried out initially from the archbishopric of Salzburg and since 830 from the bishopric of Passau. The area east of the Vienna Woods was Christianised, only then to be immediately lost to the pagan Huns in 907 and not reconquered till the late 10th century. Only then could this area, primarily settled by Bavarian colonists, permanently be made a part of the Holy Roman Empire and the margrava-

St Michael's Square in front of the Imperial Palace with Roman burial field: remnants of houses from Vindobona's suburb (2 CE)

te of Austria established. The margrave's castle was erected on the grounds of the former Roman fort. The oldest parish churches St Peter and St Rupert, existing by the 11th century at the latest, were joined by St Mary on the Bank after 1100 and St Stephen 1147.

The city acquired major significance when the margravate of Austria was transformed into a duchy and the Babenberg ruler Henry II Jasomirgott moved his residence in 1156 to Vienna, which in a few decades became the second-largest city in the Holy Roman Empire. The

new residence Am Hof was now the cultural centre of this powerful royal house. Under Leopold VI (reigned 1198–1230) the arts particularly flourished. Numerous monasteries and churches were founded, following the lead of the Scottish Monastery established in 1155. Around 1200 the city walls had to be shifted due to the sudden rise in population; Leopold's expansion of the city covered an area that was three times as large as the Roman city. The new city borders, which essentially followed the course of the present Ring Boulevard and thus encompassed today's 1st district, re-

St Rupert Church, mid 12th century, south aisles mid 14th century

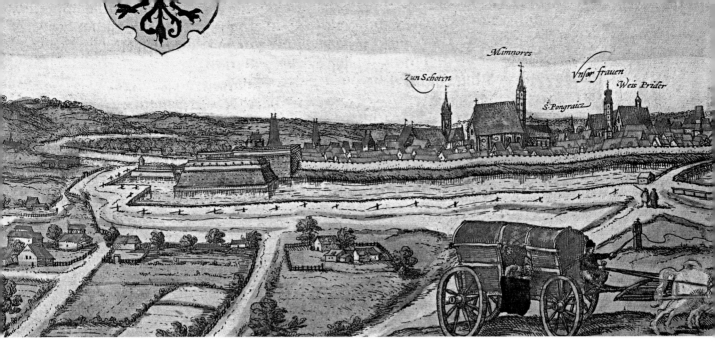

mained standing till the middle of the 19th century.

In 1246 Frederick II died without male heirs. The struggle for the succession proved to be especially conflictive and the duchy of Austria became the prized object of international politics. The Bohemian king Ottokar Premysl, who occupied Vienna in 1251, was able to finally establish himself as the ruler till his death in 1278 with the help of the provincial estates. In the legendary Battle on the Marchfeld on 26 August 1278 Rudolph of Habsburg (reigned till 1291) defeated the Bohemian king, who met his death here. Rudolph was thus able to not only make good Habsburg claims on the duchies of Austria and Styria, but also to strengthen his position in the Empire. In 1273 he had been elected – although a political outsider – to king of the Germans despite the opposition of the powerful Premyslids. The Austrian capital was now the centre of the Empire and remained in Habsburg hands for more than six centuries. Rudolph IV

(ruled 1358–65), known as the Founder, was in spite of his short reign the most colourful Habsburg of the Middle Ages. During his reign the immense nave of St Stephen was begun and Rudolph made great, though ultimately unsuccessful, efforts to elevate the church to a cathedra. Vienna was to compete just as much with Prague's St Vitus Cathedral, the chief church of the diocese formed there in 1344, as with its Charles University, established in 1348 as the first university in the empire; Vienna's own university was founded in 1365 by Rudolph. His politics are characterised by vaulting, in part widely excessive, ambitions. Even though the attempts to found a Vienna bishopric were thwarted by the resistance of the superior Bishop of Passau and the political situation after Rudolph's death became destabilised due to continuing conflicts over the succession and to divisions of territory, in many respects he laid the basis for Vienna's standing as a European centre. In artistic matters particularly the capital became a melting pot and a focus of

Archiepiscopal Cathedral and Diocese Museum, Portrait of Rudolph IV, circa 1359–65, earliest surviving autonomous portrait north of the Alps

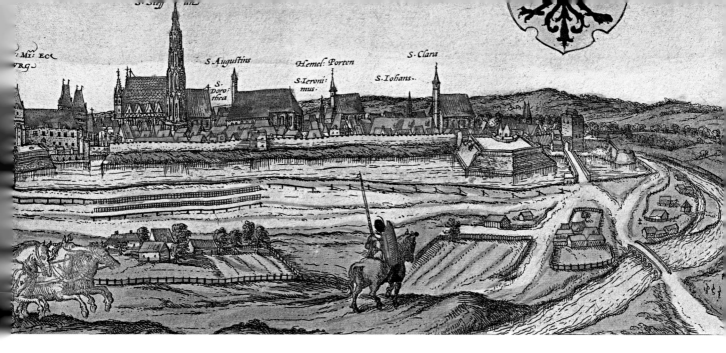

attraction: A leading position that since then it has only seldom and temporarily relinquished.

The Habsburg wars of succession which ravaged Austria after 1365 were ended by Albert V (ruled 1404–39). At first he was under the intensely contested guardianship of Leopold IV and Ernst, which was ended with the so-called Second Division of the Habsburg lands forced by the estates. This division decisively shaped developments in the following centuries: Lower and Upper Austria (with Vienna) went to Albert, Inner Austria (Styria, Carinthia and Carniola) to Ernst, Tyrol to Frederick IV from Tyrol. Albert married Elisabeth, a daughter of the Emperor Sigmund, and was declared the universal successor of the House of Luxemburg's lands – likewise with momentous consequences, as it extended Habsburg power to Hungary, Bohemia and Moravia. In 1438 he was crowned as Albert II, King of the Romans (i.e. ruler of the Germans), but died shortly thereafter in the following year during a campaign against the Turks.

Early Middle Ages

Till the 11th century the modest settlement did not expand beyond the area of the Roman castrum; as in Cologne, Trier or other former Roman cities its inhabitants lived in or among ruins. St Peter's Church was founded by Charlemagne in 792, according to legend, making it Vienna's oldest religious building. Mentioned in the 13th century as the first parish church in Vienna, St Rupert could also be a Carolingian foundation, or alternatively have been established by missionaries from Passau around 1000. Lazius states 740 as the year of its foundation and this year was repeated by an inscription on a triumphal arch in 1622. St Rupert, like St Peter, lies in the area of the Roman fort, in which small market-places had been set up among the ruins, and like St Peter was probably erected on Roman walls. St Rupert was originally surrounded by houses but today stands alone on the slope to the Danube canal to the north. The Romanesque church of the mid-12th century has survived as a

Vienna after rebuilding of medieval city walls, 1548

Old St Peter, founded by Charlemagne(?), with St Valentine Chapel (1399) and north tower, detail from a view of Vienna by Jacob Hoefnagel, 1609

simple open hall with a western tower of rubble masonry and corner ashlar; a polygonal choir was added in the 13th century and a southern aisle in the 14th. Romanesque elements in the interior include the oratory in the west, initially more modest but enlarged into a gallery with tracery balustrade under Frederick III in the 15th century, indicating the church's function as a princely church, as well as the surviving round arch window in the southern wall with partial traces of painted ashlar.

The three oldest Viennese parish churches, St Peter, St Rupert and St Mary on the Bank, were bestowed to the Scottish Monastery founded by the Babenberg dynasty in 1155 or shortly thereafter. By 1147 they had lost their function as parish churches to the recently finished St Stephen's church. Nothing has survived of the latter, the most magnificent religious building in the city with a three-aisled basilica and two eastern towers, due to subsequent alterations.

The Babenberg Period (1156–1246)

The period of the Babenberg dukes was an era of tremendous flowering of the arts. Under Leopold VI (1198–1230) Vienna evolved into a European metropolis whose extension is visible today in the course of the city walls that survived into the 19th century. In spite of many losses many buildings can still be studied in Vienna, particularly among the Lower Austrian monasteries. The centre of the court, the ducal residence,

St. Michael, Neo-classical façade by Ernest Koch, 1792, with portico from 1724 (above) and Romanesque transept (right)

Scottish Church, remnants of Romanesque basilica in the Romanesque Chapel, second half of 12th century

was erected by Henry II in 1156 on the site of the present-day square Am Hof and moved to the location of the Hofburg [Imperial Palace], probably under the last Babenberg Frederick II (1230–46). Nothing exists today of the 12th century building, while the original core of the Imperial Palace can be recognised in its oldest part, the Schweizerhof tract. Its dating is controversial, yet this type of rectangular castle with four towers at the corners corresponds to Hohenstaufen models and indicates, together with the surviving segments of walls, that it was built under the Babenbergs. A document from the 1270s however names the successor, the Bohemian king Ottokar Premysl (1251–76), as the castle's founder.

As customary in the Middle Ages, the Babenbergs endowed various monasteries and chose them as their burial places to ensure that each monastery worked for their salvation. Aside from the abbeys of Klosterneuburg, Heiligenkreuz and Lilienfeld these include the Schottenkloster [Scottish Monastery] in Vienna founded in 1155 by Henry II. The richly endowed, privileged monastery staffed by Irish Benedictines (known as Scottish monks) from St Jacob in Regensburg was initially located outside the city walls at the Freyung square in

above: St Michael, interior of nave looking east, circa 1220–50

left: St Michael, north aisle

below: St Michael, dragon capital on north crossing pier

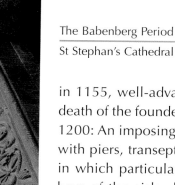

in 1155, well-advanced in 1177 at the death of the founder and consecrated in 1200: An imposing three-aisled basilica with piers, transept and crossing tower, in which particularly the three eastern bays of the aisles have survived in the outbuildings (Romanesque Chapel and Dark Sacristy) beside the Baroque choir. The southern exterior wall, the arcade to the former nave, responds, architectural sculpture and the northern portal have also been preserved. The miraculous image of the Madonna with Child in the Romanesque Chapel could similarly belong to the original décor.

The early Gothic church St Michael has been preserved to a large extent as the burial site of the city's prominent inhabitants and represents one of its most outstanding religious buildings. Vienna's enormous growth after 1200 necessitated the establishment of a second urban parish church, which simultaneously functioned as the parish church of the court. Its close vicinity to the Imperial Palace reveals that when the church was started around 1220 the relocation of the residence must have already been planned. Completed around the middle of the century, the three-aisled basilica with transept has remained almost unchanged since then, only the apse and the aisle chapels had to make way to new late Gothic structures. Babenberg architecture is in present-day Vienna hardly present. One major work however can hardly be overseen: the west end of St Stephen with the so-called Pagan Towers. One can only imagine with difficulty that the west portal, the so-called

St Stephan, Giant's Gate, left jambs, circa 1240 (above); Pagan Towers and Giant's Gate, circa 1170 and circa 1240, integrated in the façade from the 15th c. (right); Giant's Gate with re-used late Romanesque figures (below)

the vicinity of the Am Hof residence, but was integrated in the extension of the town carried out under Leopold VI. In contrast to the ambitious projects of the Viennese high Baroque, the new building from the mid-17th century incorporated parts of the older building from the venerable medieval church. This permits the adequate reconstruction of the Romanesque building begun

Laxenburg, Franzens-
burg, portal with co-
lumns from the Ca-
pella speciosa from
Klosterneuburg,
newly arranged in
1799

Klosterneuburg, Au-
gustine Canons
Church, Romanesque
building seen from
the south, 1114–36

Giant's Gate, today a bottleneck for tourists, functioned as the entrance exclusively for the church's patron or the sovereign ruler till the 18th century, with the exception of the most significant feast days, when processions marched through the Giant's Gate. The city's inhabitants entered the nave through side portals. This exclusive use must have early on lent the west end, where the royal tribune was located, a highly symbolic connotation. Only thus can the remarkable incorporation of the Romanesque structure within the immense building in the 14th and 15th century be explained, as no structural or aesthetic need existed. It was Rudolph IV especially who in the new construction from 1359 on repeatedly emphasised the link to the Babenberg period, principally at this spot.

In this way a hardly unchanged west church end has been preserved in a Gothic frame, with the oldest parts, the lower sections of the towers, belonging to building phase II, erected around 1170. The most significant elements, the portal and the western tribune, belong to building phase III, built in 1220–60 and consecrated in 1263, whose nave already possessed the dimensions of today's structure built under Rudolph in the 14th century. Various figures (lion, griffin, judge, bird) are set as spolia at the edges of the slightly protruding

Heiligenkreuz, Cistercian Church, west façade, before 1240

Heiligenkreuz, Cistercian Church, nave looking east

right: Heiligenkreuz, Cistercian Church, glass paintings with members of the Babenberg dynasty in the cloister's fountain house, 1280s

vestibule; the Giant's Gate itself is five-stepped and richly ornamented.

Closely linked to the early period of the Babenberg dynasty is the Augustine Canons foundation of Klosterneuburg north of Vienna. The Romanesque precursor of the Baroque monastery was founded and inhabited by Margrave Leopold III († 1136), canonised in 1485 and buried here. From 1113 to 1156 Klosterneuburg was the residence of the Babenburgs. Construction work on the monastery and castle initiated in 1114 must have been quickly completed, as the consecration of the church is reported in 1136. The original wall substance of the monumental basilica with westwerk, transept and crossing tower has been preserved in spite of – or maybe because of – the Baroque transformation and is visible at many spots of the building's exterior. A singular work in the style of the most modern Gothic cathedrals, possibly built by a team of French builders, is the so-called Capella Speciosa, erected around 1220 as the palace chapel of Leopold IV southeast of the monastery church. In 1799 it was dismantled and newly re-arranged in the Romantic Franzensburg in Laxenburg Castle park.

Probably the most famous artwork in Klosterneuburg is the Verdun altar, whose oldest sections were made by Nicholas of Verdun between 1171 and 1181 on behalf of provost Wernher to clad the pulpit of the monastery's church. It is a work of the most sophisticated theological content, designed according to typological principles, representing a pinnacle of medieval enamel artwork. It was reworked into a

Leopold III, it developed into the preferred burial place as well as favoured monastery of the Babenbergs. Here is where Leopold IV (1136–41), Leopold V (1177–94), Frederick I (1194–98) and Friedrich II (1230– 46) are all buried, whose foundations and gifts (Relic of the Holy Cross) were not forgotten in the monastery. A series of glass paintings in the cloister's fountain house depicting the founders was realised in the 1280s, four decades after the dynasty had died out. As in Klosterneuburg, the Habsburgs also promoted the veneration of their predecessors in Heiligenkreuz. In the chapterhouse, possibly finished before the church for the burial of Leopold IV in 1141, the tombs of the founding family were provided – likewise in the 1280s – with inscriptions and positioned in a magnificent arrangement, together other remains brought from Klosterneuburg. The centre of the Babenberg mausoleum is the altar tomb of Frederick II. At the feet of the recumbent figure two monks hold a small tablet which assumingly was used to display one of the principal and most politically significant relics in the Western world: a particle from the crown of thorns, given by Louis IX of France to the duke of Austria a few years before his death. The first monastery church begun under Leopold III shortly after 1133 initially lacked a transept, but was rebuilt in the 1140s following the Cistercian plan. At a blessing of the church in 1187 the eastern sections including the lay brother's choir in the nave were probably completed; the construction of the western bays continued for several years, yet the church was completed before the consecration of the en-

Heiligenkreuz, Chapter House, circa 1141, modified in 1240 and transformed into a Babenberg mausoleum in 1280s, altar tomb of Frederick II, after 1246, wall and vault painting with depictions of the Babenbergs buried here, 1729–30

below: Heiligenkreuz, cloister, before 1240

winged altar and enlarged, although the painters followed the Romanesque style to a remarkable degree.

Another site of the Babenberg cult is the Cistercian monastery of Heiligenkreuz in the Vienna Woods, which has survived almost unchanged since the 12th and 13th centuries. Founded in 1133 by

tire monastery complex in 1240. Nave and transept of this high Romanesque structure have been preserved, while the choir was transformed in 1288–95 into a hall choir, a masterpiece of high Gothic architecture. The cloister makes a uniform impression, the high quality in every detail making it a striking example of its kind.

The Minorite Church

The former Franciscan church is the most impressive High Gothic building in Vienna after St Stephen. The Minorite Order was invited to Vienna by Leopold VI before 1230, according to legend in 1224, and quickly engaged in an extensive range of activities that led to the foundation of an independent Austrian religious province in 1239 with its provincial minister in Vienna. On the grounds of the monastery, a private donation in the immediate vicinity of the city walls, a provisional Holy Cross chapel was first erected in which King Ottokar's heart was interred in 1278; the chapel was rebuilt as a St Catherine chapel in 1298 (no longer existing, today State Archive). The monastery with purportedly 150 monks was regarded as one of the most influential religious institutions in the city, the choir of its later church represented the most exclusive burial place in the 14th century for the higher ranks of nobility (tombs of Isabella of Aragon, Blanche of Valois, Margaret Maultasch, destroyed in 1784). The construction of the monastery was begun before 1247, the blessings of sections of the church are documented shortly afterwards. The building possessed

Minorite Church, view from southeast

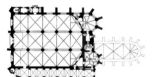

Plan of Minorite Church

Minorite Church, view from west

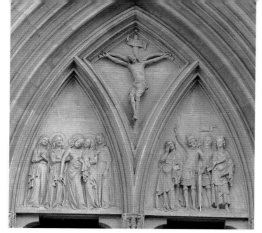

Minorite Church, north portal, circa 1330/40, with reused tympanum from St Louis Chapel, before 1328

above: Minorite Church, tympanum of right western portal, Italian sculptor, circa 1340–50

Middle: Minorite Church, tympanum of central western portal, ascribed to Brother Jakobus from Paris, circa 1340–50

Minorite Church, so-called Family Madonna with monogram of Albert II, circa 1345

right side: St Stephen's Cathedral, nave

a nave and a single aisle (following the model of the Parisian Dominican church), whose central piers today make up the southern row of columns of the present three-aisled hall church. Around 1304 the wife of Rudolph III, Blanche of Valois, planned a St Louis chapel (today dedicated to St Anthony) in the north-eastern corner of the nave, where her grandfather St Louis of France was to be worshipped. It was only realised however after 1317–28 under Isabella of Aragon, the consort of Duke Frederick the Fair, and was dedicated to her relative Louis of Toulouse, canonised shortly beforehand. Immediately afterwards it was decided to rebuild the entire church as a hall church with three aisles; the westward extension transformed the St Louis chapel into the northern aisle. The west façade was built from 1339 on, the building with its tower only entirely completed in 1390.

The huge western façade with its three Gothic portals with figures, from 1340–50 and thus the earliest in Vienna, sharply contrasts with Franciscan building practice. The sculptures, whose original polychromy was removed in 1886, are of the highest quality. Each portal is flanked by pinnacles adorned with figures. The middle portal is distinguished by its size, the Madonna on the trumeau, six jamb

sculptures, Annunciation figures in the pinnacles and a Crucifixion scene on the tympanum with the figure of the donor Duke Albert II. The overall design and the style of the sculptures of this portal, ascribed in the monastery's burial book to brother Jakobus of Paris, confessor to Albert II, are closely connected to contemporary developments in France and exerted great influence on the somewhat later architectural sculpture at St Stephen. In contrast, the tympanum of the right portal seems in its visual spatial conception to have been made by a sculptor under Italian influence. It depicts the stigmatisation of St Francis as well as the representatives of the order's three branches (saints Anthony, Clara and Elisabeth).

At this time a somewhat older St Mary tympanum was re-used in the north portal, protected since 1700 by a vestibule. It is ascribed to a sculptor from Regensburg and probably stems from the St Louis chapel constructed before 1328, depicting the enthroned Mother of God with Child with a pair of donors beside her, most probably Frederick the Fair and Isabella of Aragon.

Albert II has to be regarded as the principal client and patron of the Minorite church. His presence as witness to the Crucifixion in the tympanum of the middle portal is in itself an unmistakable signal. A further indication is his mono-

a highly modern building plan following the model of the choir erected in 1295 for the Cistercian church Heiligenkreuz. The most intensive building phase occurred in the 1330s during the reign of duke Albert II, whose monogram appears on one of the corbels under the eaves cornice. The so-called Albertine Choir was finished in 1340; its stepped, compact and clear exterior form contrasts strongly with the elegant form of the slim piers inside, on which surviving but displaced high-quality sculptures have been positioned. The division into three choirs had a specific functional reason: While the Women's Choir served the parish, the Apostle's Choir was planned as a ducal burial place and the middle choir intended for the future cathedral chapter.

A figure of major art historical significance and at the same time of widespread popularity is the so-called Madonna of the Servants, which according to a legend from the 17th century proved the innocence of a maid. The sculpture at the corner of the Apostle Choir and the southern tower hall, created around 1300 or 1320–30, is an over-life-sized sandstone figure with traces of old polychromy and must have already been intensely venerated in the 14th century.

Even before completion of the new choir the decision must have previously been taken to rebuild the nave, whose foundation stone was laid in 1359 with great pomp in the presence of Rudolph IV and his consort. The Pagan Towers were preserved unchanged, the west gallery between them given over to the newly constituted chapter and the entire western fa-

St Stephen's Cathedral, Albertine Choir, 1304–40

St Stephen's Cathedral, Madonna of the Servants, circa 1300

gram "A" on the neckline of the so-called Family Madonna in the nave. The stone sculpture dated 1330–40 represents a high-quality replica of the Madonna of the Servants in St Stephen, as well as a significant relic of the formerly sumptuous decorations that once richly filled this temple with princely tombs and altars.

Gothic St Stephen

The largest building site in medieval Vienna was located in the heart of the city. The principal parish church was the subject of the most ambitious building projects of the Habsburgs, inspired by the Babenberg aspirations plainly and continually visible in the carefully preserved Giant's Gate. In spite of all the ducal commitment and striving for prestige the gigantic Gothic building just as much represents civic self-confidence, since at least two thirds of the financing was contributed by Vienna's citizens.

In 1304 or shortly thereafter construction of the three-aisled hall church was begun,

ce of the building expanded into a wide and imposing structure by the addition of a double chapel (the so-called Ducal Chapels) to each side. The monumental, pseudo-basilican nave was constructed from the west towards the choir, enveloping the original nave from the 13th century and which was only demolished in 1426–30. The exterior walls of the aisles were finished in 1440, the sophisticated stellar vaulting in 1450. The characteristic glazed roof tiles, conceived to be seen from afar, belonged to the original building but were destroyed in 1945 together with the roof truss and replaced using original remnants.

The highly symbolic significance of this construction campaign can be measured in the strong presence of donor portraits

St Stephen's Cathedral, gable of south nave wall

left: North Tower

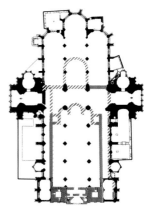

Building phases:
red = 1st half of 12th century
green = circa 1220–60
black = 14th and 15th centuries

St Stephen's Cathedral, Bishop's Door, Rudolph IV

St Stephen's Cathedral, Bishop's Door, circa 1359–65, sculptures from ducal workshop

St Stephen's Cathedral, Donor figure (Rudolph IV) on the north Ducal Chapel, ducal workshop, circa 1360–70, copy by Mathias Purkarthofer and Franz Schönthaler, 1858 (original in Historisches Museum)

St Stephen's Cathedral, south tower, so-called Primglöckleintor, 1360–70 (above), view towards middle choir (right) and Virgin of the Protecting Mantle from Albertine Choir (transferred to middle choir), circa 1330 (left)

in the south, both conical portals to which vestibules were subsequently added (Bishop's Door 1515–20, Singer's Door around 1450). Donor portraits are once more integrated in the lavish figural programmes from the ducal workshop. The Bishop's Door includes the Annunciation to one side and the donor pair in the inner archivolt, as well as coat-of-arms bearers and female saints, the tympanum the Coronation and Death of Mary. Rudolph IV holds a model of St Stephen with the east towers already planned by him, his wife wears a gown embroidered with Bohemian eagles, marking her as the heiress of her father Charles IV (a male heir was only born in 1361). In the portal's right side the so-called Coloman Stone has been set into the wall, the stone on which St Coloman allegedly suffered his martyrdom. The marble secondary relic was inserted by Rudolph as the foundation stone of the nave; a secret inscription on a buttress to one side makes an explicit reference to the donor ("dux Rudolfus fundator").

The Singer's Door depicts Moses and the Saviour outside, inside the donor pair, in the archivolts the Apostles with the Baptist and in the tympanum scenes from St Paul's life. The most famous Viennese landmark, the "Steffel", the 137m high south tower of St Stephen, was already included in Rudolph the Founder's plans, as the form of the church model held by his portrait figure distinctly demonstrates. The church however was not ultimately finished till 1433. Scholars have long disputed the identity of the architect responsible for this ambitious conception; the majority of them tend to ascribe the

on the west façade and on the side portals. On the ducal chapels are located the large-format portrait sculptures of Rudolph IV (south side) and his wife Catherine of Bohemia-Luxemburg (1342–95), replaced by copies in 1858.

In the Middle Ages the church was accessed via the two side portals, the Bishop's Door in the north and the Singer's Door

St Stephen's Cathedral, vault with view eastwards (above) and view northwest from south aisle (right)

below: Spinner on the Cross (10th District), Hans Puchsbaum, 1451–52

plans to the very young Master Michael (the surname Chnab is not verified), who received several important commissions from the dukes. Until the death of duke Albert III in 1395, i.e. for approximately 36 years long, he most likely headed the Viennese stonemason's lodge and directed the building of the tower. The competitive relationship with the Prague cathedral being erected at that time by Peter Parler is perceivable in many places. The original plan of an equivalent north tower and thus a uniform pair of eastern towers was abandoned in 1395 in favour of a much higher south tower. The insertion of the high belfry between the lower storey and the octagon is a result of this change of plans. The architects in charge till completion in 1433 (Wenzel Parler, Peter and Hans Prachatitz) all came from the Prague stonemasons lodge. The singularity of the south tower lies in its gradual diminution without almost any steps, which lends it an "appearance resembling growth" (G. Brucher) and has inspired its many descriptions as "popular tree" or "pencil" (Adalbert Stifter, Aussicht und Betrachtungen von der Spitze des St. Stephansturms, 1841). The north tower was not erected until 1467–1511.

The dominance of the stonemasons lodge from St Stephen also becomes apparent in that it was engaged for other projects, such as the so-called "Spinner on the Cross". Its location in the heavily trafficked Triester Straße is historically determined, as the ornamented column on the heights of the Wienerberg served from the beginning as a signpost on the prin-

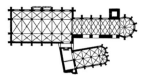

Plan of Augustine Church with St George Chapel

ciple road leading southwards. It acquired its present appearance as a result of a commission from Vienna's inhabitants in 1451/52, replacing it with a new column according to plans by Hans Puchsbaum.

Augustine Church

The Augustine church was begun in 1327, three years after its foundation by Friedrich the Fair, and built at the same time as the Albertine Choir of St Stephen. By the consecration in 1349 it was for the most part completed, except for the choir and vaulting. From the beginning it was located in close proximity to the Imperial Palace; the monastery and church of the Augustine Hermits were closely linked with the court and in part subject to decisive changes. As a result of the formal designation as the court's parish church in 1634 the church was transformed according to the Baroque style, but in 1784 reconverted to its original Gothic state in an unusual manner. In the building complex attached to its south end a St George chapel was erected in 1337–41, founded by duke Otto the Happy for a knightly order he created (Societas Templois) and since 1613 the burial place of the Harrach family.

In spite of modern usage and subsequent reforms (the west façade blocked by the east wing of the Court Library in 1769) the church, visible today only from the Augustinerstraße from the north, is recognisable as a Gothic construction, particularly in the interior. The architect of the three-aisled hall church nave was Dietrich Ladtner from Pirn (Bavaria), according to the register of masters of the Viennese stonemasons, the religious advisor the Augustine Superior General Thomas von Straßburg, while the first prior came from Bavaria.

left: Augustine Church, interior looking east

St Mary on the Bank, tower, lower four stories 1353–61, spire finished in 1429, interior looking east

St Mary on the Bank

The origins of this chapel are lost in history. It is situated on an outcrop overlooking a bank sloping to a former arm of the Danube. In the 12th century it was given to the Scottish monastery founded in 1155, destroyed in a fire in 1262 and then replaced by a new building. The present-day choir was donated by the Greif family, which owned an adjacent farm and in 1302 purchased the patronage over the chapel from the Scottish Monastery. Construction begun in 1332 and was finished by 1350, the building of the nave initiated in 1398 was completed in 1414, but a planned monastery was never founded.

St Mary on the Bank is an architectural jewel of exquisite quality. The three-bay choir ending in a 5/8 polygon stands in the tradition of the Gothic long choirs of mendicant orders' churches (cf. Minorite and Augustine churches) and indicates ties to the stonemasons lodge of St Stephen for example in the form of the interior baldachin. The walls are almost completely dissolved by means of wide, very high windows with lavish tracery, a motive emphasising the preciousness of the space consistently used for the first time at Sainte-Chapelle in Paris (consecrated 1248). The stone figures of the Annunciation and two kings from an epiphany group, the remnants of the choir's former decorations, are located at the nave's piers. The famous sculptures have been dated by A. Kosegarten to approximately 1360–65 and ascribed to the workshop of the central west portal of the Minorite church. The gestures and poses of the slightly over-life-sized figures extending

St Mary on the Bank, nave pier, angel (above) and St Mary (below) from Annunciation, circa 1360–65, originally in choir

St Mary on the Bank, plan

into the surrounding space must have made a striking impression in the brightly illuminated, dematerialised choir.

A unique consequence of the topographic location is the extremely narrow, single-aisle nave with lavish west façade and a high tower, whose openwork bulbous dome belongs to the masterworks of Gothic masonry art. The two nave portals with domed vestibules are considered original creations by Michael Chnab.

Building of the New Choir in St Michael and the "Master of St Michael"

The immediate reaction to the new choir of the city's first parish church St Stephen occurred at its second parish church St Michael, with the building of a prestigious Gothic eastern complex added to the Late Romanesque transept (preserving the old choir square). The staggered arrangement of the three apses was taken over from the Albertine Choir. Several donations (south choir 1350) indicate that the three choirs were finished by 1360. While the main and north choir have been affected by subsequent rebuilding, the south choir (Chapel of the Holy Cross and St Nicholas) remains an outstanding example of High Gothic architecture in Vienna. The architectural sculpture located here belongs to the most outstanding works from the period of 1350–55. The south choir is associated with a donation by Wernhard Schenk, who is possibly depicted with his wife next to a bust of Christ on the east wall of the transept.

On the walls of the south choir stand the stone figures of Saints Catherine and Nicholas under baldachins and on corbels with foliage. They were also donated by Schenk and provide the basis for the surrogate name of the so-called "Master of St Michael". This sculptor's monumental conception of figures imitating classical forms strongly contrasted with the ducal workshop almost contemporaneously active at St Stephen; that he originated from Italy or at least trained there is undisputed. The gown and standing pose of Catherine are unmistakeably oriented towards classical statues; with his penetrating plasticity the holy bishop could also stand in Florence.

A further figure by the same artist is the Man of Sorrows on the Singer's Door at St Stephen, dated by an inscription to short-

ly before 1367. The clearly over-life-sized figure possesses such penetrating physicality and pronounced physiognomy that it was long considered a Renaissance sculpture. This figure is an impressive example of the intensive Passion piety in the years after the great epidemic and one of the earliest public devotional images which have survived.

St Michael, view towards south choir, on the arch painting of donor pair, circa 1350 (above), St Stephen's Cathedral, Man of Sorrows on Singer's Door, Master of St Michael, before 1367? (bottom left) St Michael, St Catherine by Master of St Michael, circa 1350–55 (bottom right)

From the Late Middle Ages to the End of the Turkish Wars

History

The ground-breaking innovations in all fields of art as well as in politics made the reign of Frederick III (1440–93) the beginning of a new age for the city. The predominantly friendly relationship of his predecessors to Vienna's population turned into open confrontation, culminating in the siege of the emperor in the Imperial Palace in 1462. Divisions of territory and clashes over inheritances that repeatedly flared up under the Habsburgs weakened the economic power of Vienna and its hinterland. This was compounded by the collapse of trade with Hungary due to the Turkish invasions and the growing preference for the Brenner Pass for trans-Alpine commerce. Around 1500 Vienna was still the largest city in the Holy Roman Empire (60,000 inhabitants), but had fallen behind the wealthy cities of Augsburg, Ulm and Nuremburg and relinquished its status as a leading commercial centre. In the shadow of the south tower of St Stephen, the proud symbol of civic financial power completed in 1433, not only did the bourgeoisie lose economic power, but also its political independence to a strengthening of the city's function as princely residence. The landowning aristocracy increasingly came under pressure and ultimately their status as subjects of the Habsburgs was clearly defined. Even though these developments only became fully apparent in the course of the 16th century and are reflected for example in the expansion of the Imperial Palace or the city ordinances of 1526, their foundations had already been previously laid under Frederick III.

This same period moreover witnessed the beginning of the threat of Ottoman invasion that lasted more than 200 years. At the very latest the fall of Constantinople in 1453 made the danger for the West apparent; extensive areas of the Balkans were already in Turkish hands and the border continued to shift westwards till the first siege of Vienna in 1529. Vienna was now elevated institutionally into the "bulwark" of the Christian West. Frederick was successful in 1469 where Rudolph IV had failed a century before: the establishment of a Viennese diocese (as well as a second

left: St Stephen's Cathedral, pulpit, Anton Pilgram, 1495–98

St Stephen's Cathedral, Tomb of Friedrich III, Niclaus Gerhaert, Max Volmer, Michael Tichter et al, 1467–1515

St Stephen's Cathedral, self-portrait of Anton Pilgram, 1510–13

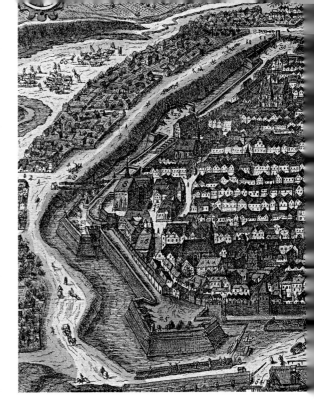

one in Wiener Neustadt) and the elevation of St Stephan to a cathedral.

Aside from its economic significance Vienna was also threatened under Maximilian I (1493–1519) with forfeiting its political role. The emperor, oriented towards the west, particularly through his marriage to Maria of Burgundy, transferred his residence to Innsbruck. After the death of the Hungarian king Louis II in 1526 the Habsburgs were once again heirs to the Hungarian and Bohemian crowns. Vienna profited from the division of Maximilian's inheritance in 1521–22 between Charles V and Ferdinand I (1521–64), since Austria and in 1526 the Jagiellon kingdoms went to Ferdinand and the city on the Danube managed as centre of the Empire to recuperate its function as capital. The siege by the Ottoman army under Sultan Süleyman II, who set off from Istanbul on 10 May 1529 and after conquering several major cities (Belgrade, Buda, Esztergom, etc.) completely surrounded Vienna on

Franz Geffels, The Relief Battle on 12 September 1683, 1688, Historical Museum of the City of Vienna

26 September, has been recorded in numerous reports and countless images. The overwhelming superiority of the besiegers (more than 100,000 against 17,000 armed men), as well as the habitual acts of cruelty committed in a war by soldiers ravaging a countryside, made the truly astonishing success of the defenders under Count Niklas Salm to be heroically transfigured in later accounts. Evidence of the continuing reverence for the commander Salm, who died as a result of a wound suffered during the defence of the Kärntnertor gate, is found in his magnificent marble altar tomb, according to the inscription commissioned (or allowed) by Frederick I, placed initially in the St Dorothea church and in 1879 transferred to the Votive church. The three-week long siege and the persistent danger posed by the Turks determined the outer appearance of the city for long. All of the suburbs were completely destroyed, the city's curtain walls to a large extent, so that the neces-

sity of erecting modern fortifications was glaringly evident. From 1530 on Ferdinand had an outer, star-shaped curtain wall with bastions constructed (ten by 1564), with a 500-step wide open space (the glacis) that was maintained unbuilt till the inner curtain wall. Till the 19th century it prevented the inner city from merging with the outer suburbs which were soon flourishing again.

The period after 1529 was characterised by confessional conflicts, only resolved in 1620 with the victory by the Catholic Counterreformation over the Protestant Bohemian aristocracy at the Battle of White Mountain. By 1550 the overwhelming majority of the population had converted to Protestantism; processions by orthodox Catholics could hardly be conducted through the streets without being disrupted and ridiculed. Only gradually were the Jesuits, brought to Vienna in 1551 by Ferdinand, able to establish themselves by means of sermons

and school instruction. In confessional issues Maximilian II (1564–76), an emperor who ardently loved the arts, took a wavering stand; Protestantism was never as tolerated, before or after him. After the demise of Maximilian and the accession of his son Rudolph II (1576–1612) the situation changed drastically for Protestants. Rudolph, who moved his court to Prague, took strict measures against the new doctrine. The outstanding figure of this policy, which was above all politically motivated (i.e. depriving the rural Protestant aristocracy of

View of the Vienna from the north (detail), 1609, copperplate engraving and etching, composed of 3 x 2 sheets, original size 795 x 1595mm. The illustration depicts the fortifications and walls of the city, for the most part completed, serving as defence against the Ottomans. Only at the Danube side is the older city wall still visible.

Marble tomb of Niklas Graf Salm, 1530–35 made for his tomb in the monastery church St Dorothea, ascribed to Thomas Hering, since disbandment of monastery in 1787 in private family ownership, in 1879 on initiative of the Wiener Altertumsverein placed in the Baptism Chapel of the Votive Church

Wiener Neustadt, former Cistercian monastery Neukloster, tomb slab of Empress Eleanor by Niclaus Gerhaert

St Stephen's Cathedral, Wiener Neustädter Altar, donated in 1447

power), and the driving force behind the Counterreformation in Vienna was Melchior Khlesl, cathedral provost and bishop since 1598, university chancellor and since 1616 cardinal. On his initiative numerous new monasteries were founded or older ones rebuilt and the Jesuits officially entrusted with the university in 1623. Under the emperors Matthias (1612–19) and especially Ferdinand II (1619–37) the anti-Protestant policy became even more severe; in 1629 Protestants had to leave properties owned by Catholics and their proportion of the population fell to a minimum.

Under Leopold I (1657–1705) all the trades and arts flourished in Vienna. The first years of his reign however were marked by the final threat from the Ottoman army, which had previously been signalled by skirmishes in Hungary years before the second siege from 14 July to 12 September 1683. The numerical forces were as lopsided as in 1529 (100,000 against 16,000), Vienna however was now defended by excellent fortifications. The military technology of the Ottomans under the leadership of the ambitious Grand Vizier Kara Mustafa Pascha had likewise improved considerably, especially the laying of mines via underground tunnels proved to be highly successful. The troops commanded by Count Ernst Rüdiger Starhemberg, although decimated by grenades and disease, defended valiantly, yet were faced with the storming of the inner wall after the Ottomans had blown up the Löbel bastion on 6 September. On the very same day the imperial relief army under Charles V of Lorraine signalled its arrival with fireworks. The Turks attempted to take the city before the army appeared, leaving the northern mountain range exposed (Leopoldsberg). From there the 65,000 strong relief army under the command of the Polish king Jan Sobieski attacked southwards before sunrise on 12 September and before the day was over was able to completely triumph over the besiegers and force them to flee pell-mell. In the main tent within the besiegers' gigantic tent city Jan Sobieski captured the inestimable treasure of the Grand Vizier. On 14 September Leopold I, who had retired to a safe distance during the siege, entered the city and had himself celebrated as victor as well as glorified in numerous pictures. During the following years further victories over the Ottomans by Charles V of Lorraine and Price Eugene of Savoy-Carignan recovered the central Hungarian plains for the Habsburgs and ultimately banished the Turkish threat.

Art under Emperor Frederick III

Frederick III not only had a special preference for precious works of goldsmith's and glass art, for gems and jewels, but also seems to have been thoroughly acquainted with current trends of a more "realistic" painting and sculpture. The employment of probably the most famous and modern sculptor in the Empire, Niclaus Gerhaert of Leyden from Strasburg, who was in Vienna since 1467 on and died in the Wiener Vorstadt sub-

urb in 1473, testifies to the aspirations and connoisseurship of the Emperor. While hardly any architecture from Frederick's epoch has survived in Vienna, some very significant works of visual art are located here, particularly in St Stephen's Cathedral. The Wiener Neustädter Altar, since 1952 in the Woman's Choir, was donated according to the inscription by the Emperor in 1447 to the Benedictine monastery of Viktring in Carinthia, but apparently set up in the Neukloster in Wiener Neustadt and purchased by the Vienna Cathedral Association in 1884. The tomb for Frederick was likewise originally not planned for St Stephan's Cathedral. The commission in 1463, probably from the Emperor and his wife Eleanor of Portugal, to create "several tombs" for the Neuklosterkirche in Wiener Neustadt, was the reason for Niclaus Gerhaert's move to Vienna. He was responsible for the conception of the tomb and for large portions of the slab for Frederick and his wife in Neukloster. Gerhaert began with the demanding work on the Adnet marble in Passau; Eleanor's stone was finished in 1467, but at Gerhaert's death in 1473 the emperor's tomb was still unfinished. In 1478 Max Vollmer was contracted to complete the tomb, the stone was brought to Wiener Neustadt in 1479 and then to Vienna shortly before Frederick's death in 1493. There Michel Tichter worked on the tomb till the Emperor was interred in the Apostle Choir in 1513. The elaborate iconographical programme depicts Frederick III in imperial insignia under an opulent baldachin on the slab framed by coats-of-arms; the side walls' reliefs represent eight episcopal and monaste-

Imperial Palace, St Mary and All Saints Chapel, St Margaret from a series of figures, Hans Kamensetzer?, circa 1470/80

left: St Stephen's Cathedral, font from 1481 by Ulrich Auer, font cover (former tester from pulpit) Upper Rhine, 1476

St Stephen's Cathedral, St Christopher, Niclaus Gerhaerts and workshop, circa 1470/80

St Mary on the Bank, Coronation of St Mary by the Master of St Mary on the Bank, circa 1460/70

below: Master of the Viennese Scottish Altar, Flight into Egypt, Museum im Schottenstift, 1469

ry foundations, alternating with the seven Electors, with saints and apostles venerated by the Habsburgs on the balustrade. Much space is dedicated to representations of animals, which can be interpreted as symbols of the demonic and ephemeral. The figure of St Christopher in the middle choir of St Stephen, formerly at the southern choir pier next to the main altar, was long considered an original work by Gerhaert. Today the majority of scholars reject this, but the design is very surely by the sculptor and the figure was probably at least carved in his workshop. At the same time another sculptor from Strasburg and close to Gerhaert, possibly Hans Kamensetzer, carved an Annunciation group and a series of saints in the Imperial Palace chapel rebuilt after 1462. The tester (sounding board) of the pulpit from St Stephen, dated to 1476 according to the inscription and used since 1947 as the cover for the font by Ulrich Auer from 1481, was also made by a sculptor from the Upper Rhine.

Viennese painting also made great strides under Frederick III. Around 1440 several artists appeared who were well acquainted with the "realism" of the Netherlands. In St Mary on the Bank two panels painted on both sides from a retable have survived that depict the Annunciation and the Mount of Olives, with the Coronation of the Virgin and the Crucifixion. The paintings made in the 1460s are not only indebted to Dutch models (Rogier van der Weyden, Dierick Bouts) for motivic details, but also for their overall composition. The most important work of this period is the high altar retable of the Scottish Church from 1469. The painters active here dealt with their models much more self-confidently and naturally than all their Viennese colleagues preceding them, colours are more clearly differentiated and help create spatial distance. A special characteristic of this artwork is the exact topographic representation of Vienna.

Art circa 1500

Based on the courtly art patronised by Frederick III a rich Renaissance art at the highest European level flourished at the turn of the century. One of the outstanding sculptors of this time was Anton Pilgram, who came from the Brno stonemason's lodge and as outsider received two of the most sought-after commissions in St Stephen: for the pulpit (1495–98) and the organ loft (1510–13). The pulpit is one of the most elaborate of its period and was most likely created in connection with the rebuilding of the rood screen. The four church doctors who look out from windows in the pulpit's body represent in a characteristic manner the four ages of man's life and the four temperaments. The "Window Watcher" beside the pulpit's base under the steps is a self-portrait of Pilgram and demonstrates, just like the church fathers, knowledge of Strasburg works. Unfortunately the work has lost much of the expressive power of its colours due to purist restorations of the 19th century. The making of the organ loft is excellently documented thanks to the conflict with the cathedral's master builder Oechsl and to three surviving drawing plans. The loft supported an organ purportedly from 1336 and removed in 1797,

St Stephen's Cathedral, Organ loft with self-portrait by Anton Pilgram, 1510–13
St Stephen's Cathedral, pulpit, Anton Pilgram, 1495–98

one of the oldest of its type. The self-portrait under the magnificently composed architecture definitely belongs to the most significant examples of psychologically perceptive Renaissance images.

Only around 1500 did Viennese painting gradually free itself from the tradition of the Scottish Monastery workshop. Lasting influence came from Lucas Cranach's stay in Vienna between 1501–03, which is not documented but can hardly be doubted in light of the clients he worked for. The 30 year-old painter from Franconia worked for the intellectual elite, painting the portrait of the rector of the university, the

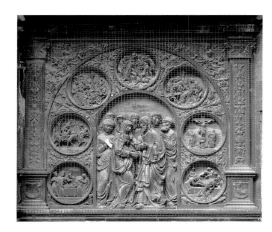

humanist Johannes Cuspinian, and his wife (Winterthur, Reinhardt Collection). The earliest dated picture by Cranach, the penitent Jerome in the Wilderness from 1502 (Museum of Fine Arts), most likely from the Mondsee monastery, certainly was painted in Vienna. All of Cranach's pictures from Vienna are distinguished by a high degree of originality. This applies to the two panels in the Academy of Fine Arts with the image of St Valentine with a donor and the Stigmatisation of St Francis, parts of the retable from the Minorite Church or from the monastery of Franciscan Observants near St Theobald on the Laimgrube. The strong dominance of landscape was further developed by the other two principal representatives of the so-called Danube school, Albrecht Altdorfer in Regensburg and Wolf Huber in Passau, who created pure landscapes. In the Museum of Fine Arts an entire room is dedicated to these works.

One of the most magnificent examples of early Renaissance architecture in the Empire, and the first such in Vienna, can be seen in the portal of the St Salvator chapel (1515–19, coat-of-arms bearer 1541).

Lucas Cranach, Stigmatisation of St Francis, circa 1502/03, Painting Gallery of the Academy of Fine Arts

Imperial Palace, courtyard of the Stallburg (residence of Archduke Maximilian), design by Jacopo Strada?, 1559–68

Imperial Palace, passage to Swiss Gate, Pietro Ferrabosco, 1552/53

Imperial Palace, Swiss Gate towards southeast, 1552/53

Imperial Palace, Ascension of St Mary Palace Chapel, choir termination, circa 1430

Of the numerous Renaissance memorial plaques that of the merchant and diocesan financial administrator Johann Straub at St Stephen's Cathedral from 1520 must be mentioned. It depicts Christ's farewell from Mary, surrounded by seven tondi with Mary's Seven Sorrows.

Imperial Palace, Swiss Wing, altered in 1549–66

The Imperial Palace before 1700

At the time of the first siege of Vienna in 1529 the Imperial Palace remained, with the exception of the Late Gothic chapel, a palace from the 13th century. Soon after the Ottoman siege was repelled, Ferdinand I moved his residence back to Vienna and initiated an expansion of the Imperial Palace together with the building of the new fortifications, which made the Palace one of the largest European residences of its time. Building continued until the early 17th century, yet the planning of almost all the buildings was done by Ferdinand I. In spite of the long period of construction the buildings are of an astonishing uniformity, in contrast to contemporary residences in Munich or Dresden. They embody a severe, almost ascetic style, similar to that preferred at the same time by the Spa-

nish line of the Habsburgs. Forms and details follow models of Italian architecture and of Serlio's treatises. The interior was modified in the 18th and 19th century, only the Swiss Wing, the Stallburg and Amalienburg have at least maintained their outward appearance from the Late Renaissance.

In 1549 Francesco Pozo began with the rebuilding of the Swiss Wing. This was followed between 1559 - 1568 by the rebuilding of archduke Maximilian's residence, known today as the Stallburg, extending towards the city centre. A third surviving complex is the so-called Amalienburg, erected from 1575 on according to plans by Ferrabosco as the residence of archduke Rudolph (from 1576 emperor) and enclosing the tournament square on the north. Building continued on it for long (1611).

Neugebäude Palace, view of main building from the north

Neugebäude Palace

One of the most enormous building projects of its time was the Neugebäude Palace, erected during 1568-87 by Maximilan II in the Simmeringer Heide (11th district) not far from the slightly older summer residence of Kaiser-Ebersdorf (1558–61 by Ferrabosco). Today's visitors primarily come to see the expressionist crematorium by Clemens Holzmeister (1921-22) on the grounds of the palace gardens, located between the enclosure walls with towers from the 16th century and opposite the main entrance to the Central Cemetery.

Neugebäude, as the pleasure palace with extensive gardens has been known since 1573, is the outstanding work of art and architecture under Maximilian II. The Emperor employed a team of fa-

Imperial Palace, Amalienburg (residence of Archdukes Rudolph and Ernst), Pietro Ferrabosco and Anton de Moys, 1575–1611 (left wing) and Imperial Chancellery wing, Joseph Emanuel Fischer von Erlach 1726–30 (tight wing)

Neugebäude Palace, enclosure walls with towers

Franciscan Church, Late Gothic Madonna (above) and façade (below), 1603-11, vestibule 1742

mous architects and decorators, above all Italians, but also Bartholomäus Spranger and Alexander Colin, who by his death had finished only the torso of the main building, yet most of the gardens.

Rudolph II had the complex continued on a reduced scale following plans by Ferrabosco; after 1600 the building suffered losses, the last in 1755 with the removal of colonnades and relief plates to the Gloriette on the grounds of Schönbrunn Palace.

The palace complex on the sloping banks of the Danube is formed into terraces; two gardens are connected by the unusually long main building (180m) with one another. The main building was built after a change in plans in 1570 and has survived as the imposing ruin of a torso. Its lower storey as well as the eastern adjacent building contain grottos, the earliest surviving examples north of the Alps. The entire complex can be regarded in all its components as the direct assimilation of Italian architectural concepts.

Early Baroque Religious Architecture

The brilliant Viennese Baroque of the period after 1700 unquestionably overshadows the achievements of the pervious epoch. Nevertheless, rare and extraordinary examples of the Late Renaissance and the Early Baroque have survived, particularly in the field of religious architecture, that above all document the development of the religious orders during the Counterreformation. An outstanding instance of the combination of Gothic and modern forms is the façade for the Franciscan Church built in 1603–11, whose gable in the forms of the German Renaissance (strapwork with volutes and obelisks) resembles a town hall, but whose window forms reveals its character as a church. Inside, the church likewise of-

Jesuit Church Am Hof, façade, F. Lucchese, 1657–62, and interior, 1607–34

fers the remarkable image of a Renaissance space integrating Late Gothic forms, despite the imposing new décor from the 18th century (especially Pozzo's high altar from 1706). The building resulted from the transformation of the medieval Penitents of St Mary Magdalene convent church from 1476. The Late Gothic image of the Virgin cleverly integrated by Pozzo in the high altar has been venerated here since 1603; it is one of the most popular pilgrimage images in Vienna.

An interesting case is the Am Hof Jesuit church, built as a Carmelite church around 1400, given to the Jesuits in

pels, embody with their lancet windows in the clerestory Gothic forms, the choir housed the Albrechtsaltar retable from 1438 (today in Klosterneuburg, Stiftsmuseum). The façade, remodelled between 1657–62 according to plans by the emperor's architect Lucchese and financed by Eleonora Gonzaga, consort of Ferdinand III, represents not just an architectural masterpiece but possibly the very first Baroque architecture in Vienna. The façade forges a relationship with the St Mary column on the square donated by the Imperial court in 1645, a true Counterreformation monument – just like the monastery itself. The stage set up between the wings of the older convent was probably used for religious plays.

A second Jesuit church was erected most likely in 1624–31, after the order took over the university in 1622, probably according to plans drawn up by G. B. Carlone. While the interior is dominated by the artistically significant transformation by Pozzo in 1703–09, the façade preserves its Early Baroque appearance, except for the towers' conical roofs (18th century) and niche sculptures (circa 1700). The square's architectural ensemble with the church, monastery buildings and the auditorium built in 1753 by Jadot de Ville-Issey unquestionably numbers as one of the most beautiful in the city. Intriguingly, the Jesuit mother church of Il Gesù in Rome did not, as one would expect, serve as the model for the Vienna Jesuit Church, but instead for the Dominican church of Maria Rotunda begun in 1631, imme-

above: Jesuit Church, former University Church, façade, Giovanni Battista Carlone, 1624–27

right: Jesuit Church, former University Church, interior, altered by Andrea Pozzo 1703–09

1554 and restored after a fire between 1607 and 1634. The Gothic structure of the three-aisled hall church with rib vaulting and octagonal piers has been completely preserved, in contrast the choir with its coffered barrel vault represents pure Renaissance architecture. The altered Early Baroque aisle walls, located before the appended side cha-

above: Dominican Church Maria Rotunda, interior looking east

above right: Dominican Church Maria Rotunda, Giovanni Giacomo Tencalla, from 1631, façade 1666–74

bottom right: Dominican Church Maria Rotunda, stucco and frescos 1650–76

Dominican Church Maria Rotunda, Ignaz Johann Bendl, memorial plaque for Georg Mittermayer († 1666)

diately after the Jesuit church. The Dominican edifice is a completely new structure built over the foundations of two medieval churches of the order, established in Vienna since 1226. The two-storey façade with gable and a central projection was raised in 1666–74 and follows the Roman model almost literally. The imposing interior was finished in its raw form by the consecration in 1634, but its décor and the scaled-down construction of the crossing dome due to building damages (a flat dome instead of a dome with tambour) was only completed in the third quarter of the 17th century. On the southeast crossing pier there is an important Early Baroque memorial plaque by Bendl with a visual language unusually emotional for the period.

In 1637 the crossing tower of the Romanesque Scottish Church collapsed. Reconstruction was immediately started under the responsibility of Antonio Carlone and Marco Spazio, from 1640 on Andrea Allio the Elder and since 1645 Silvestro Carlone directed building. The consecration took place in 1645, the décor with plaster and frescos was ap-

Scottish Church, 1637–45, west façade Filiberto Lucchese?, circa 1650 (above), interior (right) and Martyrdom of St Sebastian, altar panel in south transept chapel, Tobias Pock, 1649/50 (below)

Servite Church (9th district), from 1651, towers 1752/54, view from southwest

plied in 1648–51, while the sculpture work on the façade lasted till 1652. Without a doubt the most important church of the "Counterreformation building boom" (H. Lorenz) during the 2nd and 3d quarters of the 17th century is the

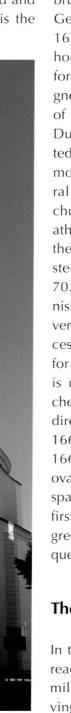

Servite church. Outside of Italy this mendicant order enjoyed little influence and lost much ground during the Reformation; with a foundation in Innsbruck in 1614 the order returned to the German-speaking territories. Since 1627 it had made efforts to establish a house in Vienna, but a contract of sale for a property in the Rossau was only signed in 1639. The initiator and financer of the church built from 1651 on was Duke Ottavio Piccolomini, who donated 48,000 guilders to the church and monastery as well as his Bohemian rural estate and moreover chose the church as his burial place. After his death in 1656 construction slowed down, the final decorations by the stucco plasterer Barberini were finished in 1669–70. With the exception of the towers, finished in 1754–56 but planned from the very beginning, and of the new altarpieces the building of the 17th century has for the most part survived. Its architect is unknown, the participation of Lucchese is speculative, while building was directed by Carlo Martino Carlone in 1661, Franz and Carlo Carnevale in 1667. The Servite church is the earliest oval building in Vienna and its interior space, an autonomous creation possibly first conceived of by Barberini, exerted great influence on the city's High Baroque architecture.

The Habsburg Crypts

In the Middle Ages the custom was already established among illustrious families of burying their dead after removing their entrails and brain, heart and

tongue. In the modern period Catholic dynasties further developed this tradition. While the embalmed body was interred in the traditional family crypt or in the church prescribed by the office of the deceased (e.g. in the bishop's church), one could by the choice of a resting place for the intestines or the heart select a monastery from which a specially intensive and permanent care for one's soul could be expected. The interment of the heart occupied a special position in such burial traditions. Of all European courts where the posthumous dismembering of the ruler was regularly carried out its practice is best known in Vienna and was continued till the late 19th century.

The "Kaisergruft" [Imperial Crypt] has existed since 1633 in the Capuchin monastery founded in 1617 by Empress Anna († 1618), the wife of Mathias († 1619), and was designated as their burial place from the beginning. Ever since the interment there of two of Ferdinand III's sons in 1639 the Capuchin Crypt has been the family burial site of the Habsburgs and now houses 146 members of the dynasty (last burial: Empress Zita 1989), including 12 Emperors and 17 Empresses. Almost all the corpses buried here had their intestines, brain, eyes and heart previously removed and interred separately. The extensive present-day burial vaults initially consisted of a simple room (Gründergruft 1633), which was repeatedly ex-

Servite Church, Interior, stuccowork by Giovanni Battista Barbarini, 1669/70

Capuchin Church, façade

Capuchin Church, Maria Theresia Crypt, sarcophagus of Maria Theresa and Francis I Stephan, B.F. Moll, 1754

panded from 1657 on, the last time in 1960–62. Daily masses celebrated there made the crypt vaults accessible to the public since 1717, at the very latest since 1753. The architectural highlights include the Leopoldsgruft, a three-aisled columned hall with a stuccoed groin vault, and the Maria Theresia-Gruft, an oval domed Rococo mausoleum. The Capuchin Crypt owes its singular place in art history however to the magnificent sarcophagi from the 18th century (Karlsgruft and Maria Theresia-Gruft). Since 1637 the tongues and hearts removed from the corpses have been interred in the Loreto Chapel of the Augustine Monastery founded in 1627 by Eleanor Augusta Gonzaga, consort of Ferdinand II, converting the chapel into the Habsburgs' "Heart Crypt".

During reconstruction of the entire church in 1784 the Heart Crypt was transferred to a new burial chamber, visible from the Loreto Chapel via two windows (last burial of a heart in 1878). Likewise in 1627, Eleonore Augusta founded the adjacent north chapel adorned with symbols of death for the "Brotherhood of the Dead" founded by her, dedicated to the burial of the executed. In 1657–58 numerous crypts and burial places were installed under the church.

The brains, eyes and intestines of the Habsburgs have been buried since 1654 in the "Entrails Crypt" in the catacombs under the St Stephen's Cathedral. By designating the so-called Old Duke's Crypt, in which a total of 17 Habsburgs had been interred between 1362 and 1566, as the repository of the

urns with the entrails, Ferdinand IV revived an interrupted tradition. In 1754–55 Maria Theresa initiated the construction of the New Ducal Crypt, to where the most significant sarcophagi and urns were translocated. The Entrails Crypt under St Stephen's Cathedral belongs to the very extensive catacombs created in 1744–52 by appropriating and rebuilding the cellars of neighbouring houses. These burial vaults are the burial site of approximately 11,000 people, including the leading Viennese Baroque architects Johann Bernhard Fischer von Erlach and Johann Lucas von Hildebrandt, until burial inside the city was banned for hygienic reasons by Joseph II in 1783. Although the vaults were restored in 1873, the sarcophagi rearranged and the bones piled up, a visit to this Baroque city of the dead today remains an exceptionally striking experience.

Capuchin Church, Charles Crypt, sarcophagus of Emperor Charles VI, Johann Nikolaus Moll and Johann Georg Pichler, 1742, 1752/53 expanded by Balthasar Ferdinand Moll

St Stephen's Cathedral, north wall of Women's Choir with portico of entrance to catacombs, 1752

Baroque Vienna (1683–1780)

History

The end of the Ottoman threat was followed by Vienna's renewed rise to a political, economic and artistic centre, as well as by remarkable urban development. Vienna grew out of its constricting medieval corset, for centuries necessary due to the external danger. The repulse of the Turks meant that Vienna once more lay in the centre of an immense empire; the extinction moreover of the Spanish line of the Habsburgs in 1700 allowed Leopold I for at least a few years to speculate with this inheritance and thus the spread of his rule to all four continents. The piety of Leopold I (1658–1705) penetrated all aspects of his reign and forged his conception of himself as emperor by the grace of God. During his reign for example St Joseph became the patron saint of the Empire in 1676. His perception of himself as Vicarius Christi on earth shaped his sponsorship of the arts and his conspicuous sense of tradition. The most distinctive example is the imposing, 14m high Pest Column at Am Graben, erected by numerous artists as consequence of a vow Leopold made during the epidemic of 1679 and consecrated in 1692. It represents not just the initial spark for the Viennese High Baroque but also the symbol of a Habsburg sovereignty founded in faith.

Leopold I was responsible for cultural decisions with far-reaching consequen-

ces, aside from his intensive promotion of Italian opera particularly the establishment of the Academy of Arts in 1692 and the appointment of the architects Johann Bernhard Fischer von Erlach and Lucas von Hildebrandt, as well as the fresco painters Sebastiano Ricci (Venice) and Andrea Pozzo (Rome). The court spoke Italian – as well as built, painted and sung in Italian: Vienna was known as the New Rome. Another aspect of Leopold's reign was the numerous noble palaces which were erected outside the fortification walls and soon shaped the image of the inner city, particularly in the Herrengassenviertel.

After his early death Joseph I (1705–11) was succeeded by his brother Charles VI (1711–40), during whose reign Vienna's social and cultural achievements reached their pinnacle. Like Joseph before him he proved to be open to art from the archenemy France, which now set the cultural tone, organising the Imperial Building Office (1716) and Academy (1726) according to Parisian models. He exhibited the Imperial paintings in the Stallburg from 1718 on and was inspired by French castles and gardens. Charles VI however also continued the imperial tradition of his father, promoted church building and from 1730 on transformed Klosterneuburg – since the 15th century the quintessence of dynastic memoria – into a gigantic residence following the model of the Spanish El Es-

Josefsbrunnen on the Hoher Markt. In 1702 Leopold I vowed to raise a memorial column after the triumphal return of his son Joseph from a battle. Charles VI had the wooden monument installed in 1706 replaced by the present one in 1732 (design by Emanuel Fischer v. Erlach)

p. 50 Trinity Column (Plague Column), designed by Johann Bernhard Fischer von Erlach and Ludovico Ottovio Burnacini, 1679–94

Mozart Memorial by Viktor Tilgner, 1896, in the Burggarten. Wolfgang Amadeus Mozart (1756–1791) moved to Vienna in 1781 and lived here till his early death

corial complex. That these were immediately stopped with his death and that the enlightened Maria Theresa showed no interest in continuing them, demonstrate how deeply rooted the conception of a Christian empire, reaching back much further than Leopold, was in Charles. He was moreover successful in elevating Vienna to an archdiocese in 1723. With Maria Theresa's ascension (reigned 1741–80) the focus of art patronage changed, as well as the manner of ruling. The bureaucratic apparatus of enlightened absolutism invaded Vienna, numerous offices and chancelleries were instituted, some in the city palaces of the deposed upper aristocracy. The Empress encouraged building on the glacis (twenty years of tax exemption for new buildings in 1767), the suburbs merged while the nobility moved further out to the surrounding towns. The university was reformed and since 1753 it was no longer in the sole control of the Jesuits.

In artistic matters Maria Theresa and her consort, Francis I Stephen of Lorraine, abandoned the Christian-ideological tradition of Charles VI. The Empress sponsored the construction of the pleasure palaces Schönbrunn, Laxenburg and Schlosshof, the making of contemporary views of the expanding city as well as pastel painting (in which she had received lessons). The exact representation of reality in Canaletto's vedute is extremely informative; they demonstrate that the former surroundings of the major noble palaces far away from the inner city were rural rather than urban.

Canaletto, Vienna, seen from Belvedere, 1758/61, Museum of Fine Arts

left: View from the Belvedere park to the Lower Belvedere and Vienna with St Stephen's Cathedral in the background

Baroque Imperial Palace Projects

The building history of the Imperial Palace is an over 600 year long history of only half or even completely unrealised new building or alteration projects. Waning interest of the rulers or a strong sense of tradition left their mark on an architectural complex unique in Europe, with building phases difficult to decipher. The last building campaign of Ferdinand I had taken place a century ago when Leopold I undertook a new attempt in 1600 to unify the palace, at its core a medieval structure. First he had Lucchese construct the so-called Leopoldine tract, connecting the old castle with the Amalienburg of the late 16th century. Another half-century passed by before work was done on the residence. Johann Bernhard Fischer von Erlach pre-

Donner Fountain at Neuer Markt, Georg Raphael Donner, 1739

Klosterneuburg, expansion of monastery to secondary residence of Charles VI by Donato Felice d'Allio and Joseph Emanuel Fischer von Erlach, 1730–40, view from east

sented an extensive urban concept in 1723 that oriented the palace along an axis towards the west and the city. The outer edge is still the broad former Imperial Stables (today Museumsquartier) beyond the fortification walls at the ou-

ter end towards the glacis. The Imperial Chancellery formed the façade towards the city, and was already foreseen in the first plans by Johann Lucas von Hildebrandt, yet built from 1726 on under the direction of Joseph Emanuel Fischer, the son of Johann Bernhard, who died in 1723. It completed the closure of the large Imperial Courtyard, which till then had consisted of only three sides. The St Michael wing with a tower towards the city was never finished.

The construction of the Imperial Chancellery was architecturally and politically explosive. The actual client, the Imperial Vice Chancellor Friedrich Karl von Schönborn, hired his personal architect Hildebrandt, who conceived of the wing as the prototype for the recon-

Imperial Palace, Leopoldine Wing, Filiberto Lucchese, 1660–67 and 1674–81

Museumsquartier, former Imperial Stables (7th district), Johann Bernhard and Joseph Emanuel Fischer von Erlach, from 1723

Imperial Palace, Imperial Chancellery, Joseph Emanuel Fischer von Erlach, 1726–30, gable sculptures by Lorenzo Mattielli

struction of the entire Imperial Palace. This extension of the plan, exceeding the authority of the Vice-Chancellor and of the architect, forced Charles VI to intervene. He ordered new plans from Fischer, the head of the Imperial Building Office, likewise for the entire complex. Hildebrandt was repeatedly defeated for decades in an architectural rivalry – much to the advantage of the buildings erected during this competitive situation – with the elder and junior Fischer. The courtyard façade of the Imperial Chancellery, a clear, classical design by Fischer, is considered one of the most mature works of this artist trained in Paris and Rome. The Baroque highpoint of the Imperial Palace complex is undoubtedly the Imperial Library, planned by Johann Bernhard Fischer since 1716,

but which was built according to Fischer's plans by his son with modifications (principally in the more Neo-Classical façade) from 1722/23 till 1734. Together with the frescos by Gran the Imperial Library represents a singular, imposing conception. The extremely complex iconographic programme of the frescos was designed by Conrad Adolph von Albrecht and is centred around the glorification of Charles VI in the central dome. The Emperor unites the strengths of Hercules with the abilities of Apollo, proving himself to thus be the ideal ruler in times of war and of peace, who raises the library after military successes. Numerous visual themes, several of them classical, allude to Charles' motto "Constantia et fortitudine", constancy (in peace) and courage (in war). This

Imperial Palace, St. Michael Wing, 1883–93

fundamental order of martial and pacific arts extends to the arrangement of the books and even to the two wings of the library, with a military façade (south) and peacetime façade (north).

Under Maria Theresa only minor modifications were made to the exterior of the Imperial Palace. She had the secular rooms redecorated à la Rococo, 1749–57 in the Leopoldine wing and 1761–64 in the Amalienburg.

Schönbrunn Palace

In their complexity the expansive grounds of Schönbrunn Palace, residence of the ruling dynasty from Maria Theresa till the end of the monarchy in

Imperial Palace, Imperial Library, Johann Bernhard and Joseph Emanuel Fischer von Erlach, 1723–34, view from Josephsplatz, altered after 1763 by Niccolò Pacassi

1918, make it a unique ensemble of buildings and gardens. No other European palace conceived as a pleasure or summer palace has enjoyed such enduring popularity among its royal house. The consequence was not only the continual growth of the collection of artworks housed in the palace, but also major renovation of the residential quarters, where today furnishings from the mid-18th century, with a very few from around 1700, are displayed solely in the exhibition rooms, and instead primarily represent the palace as the last Emperor Francis Joseph left it. Those who want to experience Schönbrunn as a Baroque and Rococo palace have to patiently bear with the obligatory Sissi tour, in order to arrive for example at the Great Gallery of the piano nobile with

Guglielmi's ceiling frescos or the adjacent Chinese Cabinet.

The architecture of the main palace however was fixed before 1696 by Fischer, who conceived of and also constructed Schönbrunn as the summer residence for the heir to the throne Joseph. Previously, in 1688/89, Leopold's court architect had presented plans for an utopian, mammoth palace in competition with Versailles (Schönbrunn I). The ground plan pictured in Fischer's "Entwurff einer Historischen Architektur" [Outline of a Historical Architecture] of 1721 was not intended to be actually built, but rather to demonstrate the "brash design ambitions" (H. Lorenz) of the architect.

Imperial Palace, Imperial Library, ceiling fresco in central oval by Daniel Gran

left: Imperial Palace, Imperial Library, interior with frescos by Daniel Gran, 1726–30, and changes after 1763 by Niccolò Pacassi

p. 60/61: Schönbrunn Palace, view with cour d'honneur and Gloriette in the background

Schönbrunn Palace

p. 63 Schönbrun, piano nobile, Great Gallery, frescos by Gregorio Guglielmi, 1760

above: Schönbrunn Palace (13th district), Johann Bernhard Fischer von Erlach, copperplate engraving by Johann Adam Delsenvah, 1719
below: Schönbrunn Palace, first design by Fischer von Erlach, 1688/89

The summer residence for Prince Joseph, begun in 1695 and at the death of the later Emperor in 1711 still unfinished, is located on a plain – in contrast to Versailles and Schönbrunn I – and built over the walls of an older pleasure palace from 1642. The severe, axially symmetric building with cour d'honneur was augmented during construction with the lateral courtyards when Joseph ascended to the throne in 1705 and a larger court had to be accommodated. Schönbrunn II has survived till today in its extension and division of floors, the façades however were monumentalised in the High Baroque sense, the central projection of the corps de logis emphasised by means of a sweeping flight of stairs to the piano nobile and a portico. Inside only the principal rooms were completed; particularly luxurious is the former dining hall, where the frescos by the Venetian Ricci from 1701/02 have been preserved on the ceiling of the "Blaue Stiege" staircase during the reconstruction by Pacassi. Since 1749 officially Maria Theresa's court architect, it was Pacassi who finished building the palace from 1745 on. While the cubature was completely maintained and Fischer's exterior structure only marginally modified, the interior rooms were completely rebuilt with full knowledge of modern French decoration systems. The immense main hall in the corps de logis occupying the entire depth of the building was sub-divided into the Great Gallery (towards the courtyard) and the Small Gallery (gardens), as well as into various cabinets. A special highlight is represented by the two Chinese Cabinets, intimate domed rooms adorned with lavish chinoiserie in 1760 (lacquered plaques, intarsia work, vases).

Around 1750 the renovation of the gardens by artists from Lorraine and Holland was initiated, beginning with the Great Parterre and the avenues, the setting up of a menagerie for exotic animals in 1751/52 and the Dutch Garden in 1753/54. Only with the hiring of Hetzendorf von Hohenberg around 1770 did the palace gardens receive their distinctive appearance with the construction of significant groups of

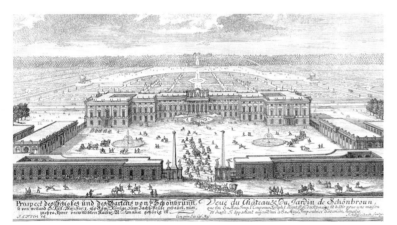

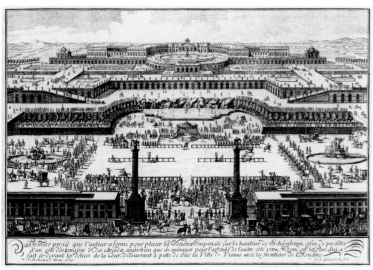

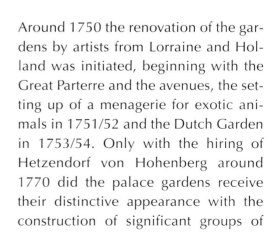

Kaunitz-Liechtenstein Palace (Bankgasse 9), Enrico Zuccalli and Domenico Martinelli, sculptures by Giovanni Giuliani, 1689/90–98

buildings. The Schönbrunn hill was now also built up, something that Fischer had already planned but till then had never been realised. Until the death of Maria Theresa in 1780 buildings and sculptures (the latter under the direction of Wilhelm Beyer) were above all installed in this section of the park, open to the public since 1779. The Gloriette (1775) not only constitutes the point de vue of the palace, but also the architectural and ideological focal point. The Obelisk Fountain (1777) contains, behind a pyramidal grotto hill with figures before a large basin, an obelisk with pseudo-hieroglyphics supported on four turtles. Near this group are the Roman Ruins, originally known as the "Ruins of Carthage" (1778).

Daun-Kinsky Palace (Freyung 4), Johann Lucas von Hildebrandt, 1713–19

Palaces

Vienna's appearance is still shaped by Baroque noble palaces, of which many were later altered but several have survived till the present day. A very limited selection of these will serve to demonstrate the variety and quality of this typical Viennese building type, possibly the most important since 1683. The prestige of the upper aristocracy essentially required a luxurious city palace befitting their social standing, as well as a garden palace with a park in the outskirts. Specific architectural traditions formed for both types. As recently demonstrated for the Palace of Prince Eugene, both buildings could establish correspondences to each other in their architectural and visual iconography. Following the lead of the Habsburgs, and occasionally even preceding them, the palaces were fitted out with artworks of all types and with ingenious fresco programmes primarily in Italian style, particularly those garden palaces erected for opulent festivities. In the city palaces the façade provided the best stage for self-glorification by means of sophisticated architecture and elaborate sculptural groups. It comes as no surprise then that noble palaces made up a large share of the oeuvre of the most famous Viennese architects such as Martinelli, Fischer or Hildebrandt.

The Kaunitz-Liechtenstein palace begun in 1689/90 according to plans by the Munich court architect Zuccalli and the Roman Martinelli for Count Dominik Andreas Kaunitz occupies a special place historically. The building, regarded as the first work of High Baroque architecture in Vienna, and sold to the Italophile noble Johann Adam von Liechtenstein during its construction in 1694, faithfully follows urban Roman models, in particular Bernini's Palazzo Chigi-Odescalchi from 1664. The façade's design with colossal pilasters emphasising the central projection and the monumental middle portal adorned with sculptures defined the prototype for Viennese city palaces. Just as pioneering was Fischer's city palace erected for the military hero Prince Eugene of Savoy from 1696 on; its famous interior décor in the Parade Rooms, above all in the staircase, have been preserved, although the building's present-day function as a Ministry makes access difficult.

In the following years the city palace evolved into the most ambitious building type for the new and old aristocra-

above: Civic Arsenal, today Fire Service Office (Am Hof 10), Anton Ospel, 1731/32, sculptures by Lorenzo Mattielli

left: Trautson Palace (7th district, Museumsstraße 7), Johann Bernhard Fischer von Erlach, 1710–12, main façade

Liechtenstein Palace (Museum, 9th district, Fürstengasse 1), Domenico Egidio Rossi and Domenico Martinelli, 1690–1704, courtyard façade from the south

cy. An unusual solution is represented by the palace on the Freyung square built following a design by Hildebrandt between 1713–19 for Count Wirich Philipp Daun, Viceroy of Naples. The extremely long property with two interior courtyards presented a challenge for the planning of the required series of lavish rooms, yet because of its location on a square offered the rare opportunity of erecting a façade visible from a distance. The staircase by the decoration artist Beduzzi belongs to the most impressive of its type. It combines works of sculpture, in particular the high-quality putti on the balustrade by Kracker with a ceiling fresco, an early masterpiece by Carlone.

Public buildings and chancelleries erected in the early 18th century followed the city palaces as regards façades and

their urban impact. The Imperial Bohemian Chancellery, built between 1709–14 according to Fischer's design and expanded by ten axes to the Fütterergasse as well as by one axis to the Jordangasse in 1751–54, is a free-standing building whose façade however partly lies in narrow lanes, but does not differ in any way from an aristocratic palace. The Bürgerliches Zeughaus [Civic Arsenal], created by reconstructing and uniting several previous buildings by Ospel (1731/32), is unusual in the design of its façade. The double-headed eagle with Imperial crown and the impressive sculptures on the parapet allude to its function as a repository of weapons.

The dense garland of garden palaces near the city (in the 18th century more than 180 were built) is a specific Viennese phenomenon and a consequence

Liechtenstein Garden Palace, Hercules Hall, designed by the architect Domenico Martinelli shortly after 1700, fresco by Andrea Pozzo (1642-1709) with Labours of Hercules and his Apotheosis, 1704-1708

Golden Wagon of Joseph Wenzel I of Liechtenstein, 1738, Nicolas Pineau (1684–1754), newly exhibited in the Sala Terrena of Liechtenstein Garden Palace in 2003

Upper Belvedere,
from 1720/21, view
from south

of maintaining the glacis unbuilt for centuries. Here, directly before the gates of the city, the leading noble families were able to impressively demonstrate their patronage on their large properties. One of the first was the powerful noble Johann Adam Andreas von Liechtenstein, who purchased a lar-

ge property on the Rossau and immediately sought out an architect, if possible Italian. A traditional, severe design by Rossi was realised from 1690 on and completed with slight modifications under the direction of Martinelli. The opulent, excellently conserved murals of the palace are outstanding and were execu-

ted – with an important exception (the frescos in the staircase and ground floor by Michael Rottmayr, 1708) – by Italians: the fresco "Apotheosis and Deeds of Hercules" in the Great Hall of the piano nobile by Andrea Pozzo (1704–08), who had just finished the Jesuit church, and the residential rooms by Marcantonio Franceschini (1709), the leading painter of Bologna. The Italian impression is completed by the extensive collection of paintings and garden sculptures by Giovanni Giuliani.

A different character is displayed by the garden palace near the Inner Ring Bou-

Belvedere

Upper Belvedere, Marble Hall, ceiling fresco with apotheosis of Prince Eugene by Carlo Carlone, quadrature by Gaetano Fanti, 1721–23

Upper Belvedere, view from the west

levard built according to Fischer's plans in 1710–12 for the Imperial Chief Steward Johann Leopold Trautson. Fischer studied the forms of contemporary Palladianism, which offered a variety of neo-Classical solutions for rural palaces. The quintessence of the Viennese garden palace however is surely the complex erected for Prince Eugene of Savoy by his preferred architect Hildebrandt, the Lower (from 1714) and Upper (from 1720/21) Belvedere. The two palaces connected via a garden represent conceptually and artistically the pinnacle of Viennese garden palaces. The smaller Lower Belvedere, broadly laid out, relatively simple and integrating the function of an orangery, served the iconographically ingenious promotion of the war hero of small stature, as the large marble banqueting hall (ceiling fresco glorifying the Prince by Martino Altomonte and Marcantonio Chiarini, 1715–17), the gallery and the lavishly decorated residential rooms demonstrate. The more significant building however is the Upper Belvedere, set on a hill to the south and in which message and extravagance culminate. The exterior alone announces this by means of a dynamic façade, corner pavilions and an opulent programme of sculptures. The equilibrium of the architectural forms, the inventive positioning of the sculptures and the high quality in every detail testify to the connoisseurship, to the unlimited financial resources but also to the obligations of self-promotion of the "foreign" Prince. The interior, to a great extent de-

right: Upper Belvedere, staircase, stuccowork by Santini Bussi, 1722/23

Belvedere garden

Palace of Prince Eugene of Savoy (Austrian Gallery, 3d district), Johann Lucas von Hildebrandt, Lower Belvedere, from 1714

Belvedere/Hetzendorf Palace

signed by the decoration specialist Claude le Fort du Plessy, fulfils all the promises made by the exterior. The most impressive rooms are undoubtedly the luminous staircase covered with exquisite white stucco and the adjacent marble hall. There Hildebrandt's architecture dissolves at the heights of the mezzanine windows in the skilfully painted quadratura architecture by Fanti, to ultimately culminate in the ceiling fresco by Carlone. Only a bit more modest is Hetzendorf Palace, whose present size resulted from its alteration into the retirement residence of Charles VI's widow Elisabeth in 1743–45. Yet already before this expansion following plans by Pacassi, Maria Theresa's court architect, Hetzendorf had produced a highly significant building exemplifying the escape of a portion of the aristocracy to the suburbs. A first building by Fischer for Count Sigismund Thun was altered according to designs by Ospel and Beduzzi for the Liechstenstein family before 1719. The façades are from this period as well as the mythological sculptures of the courtyard front (1715/17, ascribed to Lorenzo Mattielli). Inside the spectacular décor has been preserved, particularly in the Main Hall in the piano nobile, completely painted by Messenta and Carlone.

Hetzendorf Palace (12th district, Hetzendorfer Straße 79), Johann Bernhard Fischer von Erlach, Anton Ospel, Antonio Beduzzi, from 1694, 1715–19, modification by Niccolò Pacassi 1743–45, central projection from courtyard façade

right: Lower Belvedere, Marble Gallery around 1940

St Roch Church (3d district), rebuilt 1687, façade 1718–21

High Baroque Religious Architecture

In 1683 the suburbs with their churches and monasteries were for the most part destroyed. Their reconstruction led to interesting solutions, generally eclipsed by the important churches of the following generation. One example is the St Roch church on the Hauptstraße in Landstraße rebuilt in 1687, originally the monastery church of the Discalced Hermits of St Augustine summoned to Vienna from Prague in 1630. While the prominent double tower façade is a later addition from 1718–21, the interior provides a rarely uniform image of the early years after the second Turkish siege. The prominent coat-of-arms cartouche on the chancel arch's crown and particularly the magnificent high altar-piece, donated in 1689 by Leopold I, indicate the strength of the imperial commitment. Peter Strudel's retable depicts St Mary and plague saints, including the church's patron St Roch, alluding to the constant threat of epidemics (e.g. in 1679 and 1713).

A highlight of European Baroque architecture is the new church of St Peter in the city centre, begun in 1701 by Gabriele Montani and completed by Hildebrandt between 1703 and 1722. The principal façade with short towers, together with the high dome, fits exactly into the row of houses on the Jungferngasse, so that a type of cour d'honneur is formed. From St Stephen's Cathedral the steep dome sets an effective accent. In spite of the pre-determined reduced dimensions (hardly 50m) the extreme

St Roch Church, interior with high altar, donated in 1689 by Leopold I

height and compactness of the dynamic building achieves a monumental effect. The basic arrangement of the interior with its emphasis on the diagonals was created by Hildebrandt, its further conception however carried out under the direction of Steinl; here the architectural emphases are replaced by a vigorous decoration style. The pinnacle is Rottmayr's many-figured ceiling fresco of the Coronation of St Mary from 1714/15.

About 1727–30 the choir and high altar were created by Antonio Galli-Bibiena and in 1751/53 the vestibule with the important sculptures by Franz Kohl.

Shortly afterwards St Charles was erected, after St Stephen's Cathedral probably the most famous church in Vienna, today as well as at its inauguration. When the steep domed oval space of St Peter suggests more an advanced artwork

above left: St Peter, Johann Lucas von Hildebrandt, 1701–22, southwest façade

above right: St Peter, Johann-Nepomuk-Altar, Lorenzo Mattielli, 1729, and view from the east

the high drum-dome with the antique motif of the two relief-covered triumphal columns, which simultaneously refer to Charles' personal motto "Constantia et fortitudine", the columns of Hercules (world dominion), Solomon's Temple and Charles' title as "Emperor of Peace" (Peace of Rastatt 1714, end of the conflict with France). The relief frieze spirally running up the columns (Johann Baptist Mader, Johann Baptist Straub, Jakob Schletterer, 1724–30) depicts the life of the church's patron St Charles Borromeo, the crowning eagles are the work of Mattielli. The gable of the columned portico bears a relief with the representation of Vienna's rescue from the plague through the intercession of St Charles, above it a sculptural group with his apotheosis (Stanetti). The personifications of Religion, Charity, Penitence and Piety on the parapet (Mattielli) as well as of Faith and Hope on the conical roofs of the lateral towers represent the monument's universal Christian aspirations.

Inside the visitor's gaze is drawn upwards by the elder Fischer's clear and balanced architecture to where initially a coffered dome was planned, which would have underlined the temple-like, monumental character of the building. Under Fischer the Younger this severity was moderated and the interior adorned in 1725–30 with frescos following an iconographical programme by the imperial advisor Conrad Adolph von Albrecht. The large fresco of the oval do-

p. 77: St Peter, interior towards choir, décor following plans by Matthias Steinl, from 1714

St Peter, frescos in oval dome, Johann Michael Rottmayr, 1714/15

than a parish church, then St Charles is in every aspect "more monument than church" (H. Lorenz). The church is a votive building, erected by Charles VI after a pledge made following the plague of 1713, and which provided the occasion for a highly complex programmatic work. Between the wide mock façade, oriented towards the north to the Imperial Palace, and the extremely steep oval dome there is hardly any physical connection; both are independent, self-enclosed architectural components. The façade combines the Baroque motif of

St Charles Church, façade with gable relief of the rescue of Vienna from the plague thanks to intercession by St Charles Borromeo and group of figures with his apotheosis, Giovanni Stanetti, 1725

me shows the intercession and virtues of St Charles. The choir is dedicated to the glorification of St Charles Borromeo; it was planned by Fischer senior, but only decorated in 1728/29, together with the high altar (model by Ferdinand Brokoff).

A third Viennese religious building of the High Baroque is world famous, the "Maria Treu" [St Mary Faithful] of the educational order of the Piarists begun in 1716 in the Josefsstadt. The order established itself in Vienna in 1697 on the initiative of Marquis Malaspina and first constructed a chapter house there. The church expresses the basic conception of an acutely curved oval, veiling the transition to a flat dome. This dissolving of architectonic boundaries, a characteristic of the Bohemian Baroque of the period, was hardly present in Vienna,

before as well as after. Since building plans and archival documents are missing, the identity of the architect is unknown. The completion of the church, in 1731 still lacking its dome, was accomplished according to plans by Gerl in 1750. The façade with two towers reveals the curvature of the interior, in the ground plan an octagon with the sides curved inwards, consisting of alternating deep and shallow chapels. The frescos and altar decorations were completed from 1752 on.

The murals of the main dome and the side chapels are the first frescos by one the most important Austrian painters, Maulbertsch, at that time only 28 years old. The frescos particularly have won the Piarist church its reputation as the most beautiful Baroque church in Vienna. They depict the Mother of God surroun-

St Charles Church, dome

St Charles Church, interior looking towards choir

p. 79: St Charles Church, façade

St Charles Church, choir with high altar, Johann Bernhard and Joseph Emanuel Fischer von Erlach, model by Ferdinand Brokoff, Glory of St Charles Borromeo, 1728

St Charles Church, ceiling fresco, Johann Michael Rottmayr, 1725–30, Intercession by St Charles Borromeo

ded by key scenes from the Old and New Testaments and by current saints, such as the order's founder Joseph of Calazanz and the Dominican Thomas Aquinas.

Pilgrimage Churches

Less known as these milestones of art history are the numerous pilgrimage churches in Vienna, which after 1683 once again flourished and in the 19th century were still the goal of picturesque popular festivals. The objective of pilgrimages to Mariabrunn [St Mary's Well] was an image of St Mary that according to legend was drawn from the water twice, first from the Wienfluss river and later from a well. Ferdinand II donated the simple chapel in 1636 to the order of the Discalced Hermits of St Augustine (since 1630 in Vienna, cf. St Roch), who had a new building and a monastery complex erected by Carlone between 1639 and 1655. As an imperial pilgrimage church it was richly endowed and after its destruction in 1683, almost certainly only moderate, immediately rebuilt. Today it remains, in its appearance and in parts of its interior décor, a building from the mid-17th century. The portal ante-structure and the high-quality altarpieces though were added around 1730. The most spectacular artwork in Mariabrunn is the Holy Theatre in the Wies Chapel, erected in 1723 next to the choir. The chapel moreover houses seven paintings with the foundation legend (1736) and a copy of the Upper Bavarian "Wiesheiland" figure of Christ of the Flagellation (1760). The Theatre from around 1750 is one of the few surviving religious Baroque stages, on which canvas scenery

right: Piarists' Church Maria Treu (8th district), Johann Lucas von Hildebrandt and Matthias Gerl, 1716–31 and from 1750, façade

and life-size figures from Nativity and Passion plays, so-called "Kontursägebilder" (painted wooden boards with sawed-out outlines), could be placed. The Theatre otherwise resembles a large Baroque opera stage. The combination with a Holy Sepulchre is unique, in which a figure of Christ in the Sepulchre (also preserved) could be placed.

Maria Lanzendorf, south of the city limits and close to the imperial hunting lodge of Laxenburg, likewise received ardent attention from the Habsburgs. The 15 documented visits by Leopold I to the construction site, his financial support and the many stays of his successors, including Maria Theresa, testify to the status of Maria Lanzendorf as one of the most important modern pilgrimage sites of the imperial house. Correspondingly, the architecture and décor of the complex are of the highest quality and conceptually intriguing. A Marian pilgrimage site is already documented in 1349 for the parish church, which in a chronicle from 1744 is traced all the way back to Charlemagne. The idea of venerable age possibly played a role in the decision (likely by Leopold I) of letting the Gothic choir remain standing in the huge new Baroque building. This form of conservation of the old church is probably most due to the fact that the pilgrimage image, a Late Gothic Pietà, was destroyed in 1683 and had to be replaced with a copy. Since the choir was regarded as ancient, it now assumed the aura of authenticity lost by the actual religious image. Another alteration of the Baroque choir in 1723–31, made necessary by an increase in the number of pilgrims, reinforced the situation of the free-standing structure within the church space, adorned with Baroque ornaments yet plainly recognisable as a medieval building. The enormous prestige of the complex is demonstrated by the participating artists, the architect Steinl and especially Rottmayr, whose ceiling fresco from 1728–30 (the last work of the elderly master) was destroyed in 1945, but whose high altarpiece (Mount of Olives, 1730) and the left choir altar panel (Stigmatisation of St Francis, 1730) have been conserved.

South of the church is the spectacular calvary laid out by the Franciscan brother Niering in 1699. The artificial hill made of bricks and plaster is built over an oval chapel and mounted via a narrow stairway. One climbs by several grottos, in which carved wooden figures from the Passion are displayed, reaches the top and stands at the foot of a stone Crucifixion. Continuing southwards, one passes an imitation of the Scala Santa, the Holy Stairs (built in 1709). The conclusion of this procession is a copy of the Holy Sepulchre in Jerusalem.

Mariabrunn Pilgrimage Church (14th district), Domenico Carlone, 1639–55, portal ante-structure and sculptures 1729

Mariabrunn Pilgrimage Church, interior, high altar with devotional image, circa 1730/35

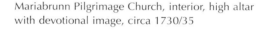

Mariabrunn Pilgrimage Church, Holy Theatre in the Wies Chapel, circa 1750

Maria Lanzendorf Pilgrimage Church, calvary, Franz Niering, 1699

In the immediate vicinity of Vienna's inner city, not to be overseen when approached from the Westbahnhof train station, is Mariahilf [St Mary Aid], one of the most distinguished Viennese pilgrimage churches, directly linked to the victory over the Ottomans. A simple chapel under the supervision of the Barnabites with a painting of St Mary (1660, one of the many copies of the famous devotional image by Lucas Cranach), which had previously been put in safekeeping, was destroyed in 1683. For the return of the painting, believed to be connected with St Mary's intercession

Maria Lanzendorf Pilgrimage Church (Lower Austria), Matthias Steinl, 1699–1703, view from southwest

Mariahilf Pilgrimage Church (6th district), façade,
Franz Jänggl, 1715–23

for the military victory, a new church
was erected by Sebastiano Carlone in
1686–89. It was modified by Jänggl in
1711–15, the towers' conical roofs were completed in 1721–23, the façade's
sculptures installed in 1724. Artistically, the building is not exceptional, its
décor however is sumptuous (high altar
by the Salzburg artist Mösl (1757), altar-
piece by Paul Troger (1760) and paintings by Rottmayr (circa 1700).

above right and be-
low: Mariahilf Pilgri-
mage Church, interior
towards the south,
1711–14, high altar
with devotional image
of Mariahilf, Sebastian
Haupt and Jakob
Mösl, 1757

Classicism, Romanticism, Biedermeier

History

The period between 1780 and 1848, from the death of Maria Theresa to the ascension of Francis Joseph, was marked in Vienna as elsewhere by fundamental political and social cataclysms, which hinder any notion of a homogeneous epoch. Joseph II (1780–90, from 1765 co-regent with his mother) was especially in the first years of sole rule a radical reformer: He closed down two thirds of the territory's monasteries, all of the church's assets, including those of the bishoprics (35 million guilders), were transferred to a "Religious Fund", parishes re-structured and masses regulated. Joseph banned most of the popular pilgrimages and processions, removed Baroque décor from Gothic churches, meticulously dictated the sober rites of masses and burials and ordered the closing of all cemeteries inside cities as a hygienic measure. Josephism meant a break with religious tradition. As a result of massive resistance on the part of the population many of the regulations had to be rescinded.

After the brief intermezzo of the revolution's sympathiser Leopold II (1790–92), Francis II (1792–1806, as Francis I Emperor of Austria 1804–35) set a conservative and strictly absolutist course. With Napoleon's victory (Emperor of France on 18 Mai 1804) the direct threat to Austria and the Roman Imperial crown increased. On 11 August 1804 Francis ac-

cepted the title of "Emperor of Austria", thus anticipating the dissolution of the Holy Roman Empire in 1806. In winter 1805/06 and in 1809 French troops we-

above and below: Imperial Crown and Imperial Cross with Holy Lance and Particle of the Holy Cross. These costly medieval goldsmith works belong to the Imperial Jewels (also known as Imperial Insignia or Treasure), the insignia of sovereignty of the emperors and kings of the Holy Roman Empire. In 1800 or 1801 they were brought to Vienna to protect them from the advancing French troops and are preserved today in the treasury of Vienna's Imperial Palace

p 86: Antonio Canova, Burial monument for Archduchess Marie Christine in the Augustine Church, planned 1798, realised from 1800 on, installed 1805

re twice successful where the Ottoman besiegers had failed: in occupying Vienna, in 1809 particularly not without destruction.

After Napoleon's conclusive defeat the restructuring of Europe was worked out at at the Congress of Vienna in 1814/15. Vienna occupied at this time a leading political position, which during the Coalition Wars it had not always occupied. Austria under Francis I and his premier

St Michael's Church, Jean Baptist d'Avrange, high altar, 1781/82

politician Prince von Metternich (1773–1859), represented, as a state determinedly set on restoring the old order, a guarantee for the maintenance of the reinstated status quo. Restrictive measures, an effective police apparatus and the tight organisation of ministries characterised domestic policy, which did not earn the Emperor much favour with his subjects (and less with subsequent historians). Ferdinand I followed his father on the throne (1835–48, † 1875), although his inability to rule due to a weak constitution was apparent. Till his abdication the de facto ruler was the State Conference, a government cabinet of four including Metternich.

On 13 March 1848 the enormous social tensions exploded; dissatisfaction reigned among the wealthy yet politically disfranchised middle class, the students repressed by the iron censorship of the press and particularly the underclass in the suburbs, impoverished by mass unemployment. The outcome of the violent fighting, during which the military, ministries and factories were attacked, was the formation of a Revolutionary Guard, whose principal demands were freedom of the press and general suffrage. Metternich escaped to England. On 22 July a parliament was created representing all the classes. The united front of National Guard, students and workers however broke up in the face of the general crisis; the political reaction succeeded after bloody fighting in smashing the provisional government in October. Ferdinand I, at no time a target of the attacks, but who nevertheless fled to Olomouc, renounced the throne on 2 December in favour of his 18 year-old nephew Francis Joseph. Despite the failure of the revolution the year 1848 marked the end of the strict repression of Metternich's era.

Style Pluralism before 1800

In possibly no other city in the last two decades of the 18th century did contrary idioms of style thrive in such proximity and with such similar intentions as in Vienna. The renovation and re-decoration campaigns of three of the most important and highly traditional churches, the St Michael, the Augustine and Minorite temples, mock all attempts at a linear evolution of style. The Barnabite order, since 1626 possessor of St Michael, had the high altar – not yet 30 years old – replaced in 1781/82, in order to appropriately present the devotional image of the Maria Candia icon, till then displayed on a separate altar. D'Avrange, Vice Director of the Academy of Engineers at the Laimgrube, completely re-designed the entire chancel, a conception which can only be inadequately described as the culmination of Baroque altar architecture. In contrast to the competing design, d'Avrange uncovered the medieval choir windows till then walled up and used the existing Gothic wall divisions and profiles, so that it is hardly surprising that the publication on the occasion of the consecration (1782) speaks of "Gothic taste". Nevertheless, stuccowork (Karl Georg Merville) and the integration of the entire altar space is the purest High Baroque, the sculptures however more tran-

High altar of the Minorite Church, Johann Ferdinand Hetzendorf von Hohenberg, Altar panel: Angels carry the devotional image Salus Populi Romani from Santa Maria Maggióre in Rome, Christoph Unterberger, 1786

quil and early Neo-Classic. In 1784 Joseph II ordered the elimination of all Baroque elements from the Augustine church (the monastery was disbanded in 1783) and did not even balk at destroying all the altars and epitaph me-

Minorite Church, interior, altered y Johann Ferdinand Hetzendorf von Hohenberg, 1785/86

Fries-Pallavicini Palace (Josefsplatz 5), Johann Ferdinand Hetzendorf von Hohenberg, 1783/84

Augartenportal (2nd district), Isidor Carnevale, 1775

is provided by the burial monument planned for the Archduchess Marie Christine, commissioned by her consort Duke Albert of Saxon-Teschen in 1798 and installed in the church, one of Canova's major works and a true manifest of neo-Classical monumental sculpture and illusionist pathos. The highly symbolic mock pyramid possesses a simulated tomb entrance, to which an allegorical funeral procession advances. An even more rigorous neo-Gothic transformation was performed in 1785/86 on the church (today the national Italian church) of the Minorite order (transferred in 1783 to the Josefstadt), likewise under the direction of Hohenberg. The choir was walled up and converted into a block of rental flats, the important tomb monuments removed, the east end of the hall church's nave rounded off, the wall divisions unified and freed of all images. Hohenberg's high altar is a singular conception in which Baroque elements certainly have their place. The same architect built a city palace on the Josefplatz in 1783/84 for Johann Graf Fries, a thoroughly neo-Classical building opposite the Imperial Library by Fischer von Erlach.

morials. The renovation was carried out under the direction of the chief court architect Hohenberg, a pioneer of Historicism, whose oeuvre is marked by stylistic pluralism – or rather adaptability: Under Maria Theresa he designed Late Baroque buildings for Schönbrunn (Theatre 1766, Gloriette in the park 1773), under Joseph II neo-classical (Austerlitz 1786) and neo-Gothic churches. Hohenberg had the Augustine church completely whitewashed and altered wall divisions and columns. The church thus appears as though the medieval building were transformed back to its legitimate state. A radical contrast

Joseph II's leading architect however was Isidor Carnevale, originally from Paris and the Emperor's imperial architect before 1780. In his early period at least he advocated a radical revolutionary architecture, manifested above all in the Augartenportal (1775). Here a triumphal arch with a massive attic is penetrated by triple archways and flanked by rusticated guardhouses. The Josephinum is regarded as Carnavale's fore-

most work, built in 1783–85 for the Medical-Surgical Military Academy in the proximity of the General Hospital. The so-called Fool's Tower (1783/84), a castle-like, five storey circular edifice, is in its compactness an unusual example of revolutionary neo-Classicism and can most likely be ascribed to him as well.

Architecture of the First Half of the 19th Century

Emperor Francis had new city gates constructed, of which the Äußere Burgtor [Outer Castle Gate] was preserved in the posterior planning of the Emperor's Forum. Nobile took over the project planned in 1821 by Cagnola and reworked it in the style of Carnevale's revolutionary neo-Classicism. He reversed the customary distinction between city and field façades, by making the inner façade richer than the outer one – an understandable decision in light of

the loss of the gate's function as a fortification, and at the same time characteristic of architecture since the 18th century and its orientation towards the

Josephinum, today Institue for the Histroy of Medicine (Währinger Str. 25, 9th district), Isidor Carnevale, 1783–85

left: Narrenturm [Fool's Tower] of the General Hospital (Pathological-Anatomical Museum, 9th district), Isidor Carnevale, 1783/84

Äußeres Burgtor gate, Luigi Cagnola und Pietro Nobile, 1821–24, Ring Boulevard front

Theseus Tempel, Volksgarten, Pietro Nobile, 1819–23

above left: Clam-Gallas Palace (French Cultural Institute), former Dietrichstein Palace (Währinger Straße 30, 9th district), Heinrich Koch, 1834/35

above right: Scottish Monastery, façade towards the Freyung, Josef Kornhäusel, 1827/28

city centre. Nobile also designed the Theseus Temple in the neighbouring People's Garden (1819–23). The temple, an imitation of the Theseion in Athens, was conceived as a public museum of antiquities and erected on occasion of the purchase of the marble sculpture group "Theseus slays the Centaurs" by Antonio Canova, commissioned in 1805 by Napoleon for Milan. The sculpture was now politically re-interpreted as representing the victory over Napoleon.

In this period the administration building increasingly gained significance as an architectural type. Often the compact buildings were ennobled with motifs from palace architecture, the neo-Classical repertoire of forms simplified and décor for the most part not used. The leading representative of Viennese Biedermeier architecture was Kornhäusel. In 1826 he received the commission for the extensive renovation of the old Scottish Monastery; its façade towards the Freyung square is characteristic of Kornhäusel's reduction of the colossal order and separation of a building's components. In the last years before the 1848 Revolution the building scene was dominated by Sprenger, since 1842 head of the Imperial Building Office. Buildings such as the Mint (1835–38) demonstrate Sprenger's quality, who understood better than all his contemporaries how to provide an appropriate, economical design satisfying functional demands without exceeding financial restraints.

The traditional building types of the 18th century, palaces and churches, were not completely abandoned. The Albertina, directly adjacent to the Imperial Palace complex, was created by enlarging a Late Baroque palace in 1801–04 for Duke Albert of Sachsen-Teschen, the son-in-law of Maria Theresa. Aside from residential quarters the palace also housed the graphic collection of the duke, the nucleus of today's world famous museum. In spite of several rebuilding campaigns Montoyer's simple neo-Classical façades are still recognisable, naturally under the superimposed

Mint (Am Heumarkt 1, 3d district), Paul Sprenger, 1835–38

ALBERTINA

Dürer's Hare on the cover of "Great Masters of the Albertina"

Albertina, former palace for Duke Albert of Sachsen-Teschen, since 1918 museum, Louis Montoyer, 1745/47, current state 1801–04, 1822/23 and 1865–67, flying roof by Hans Hollein, 2001–03

Neo-Baroque forms. The principal building by this architect is the Rasumofsky palace (1806/07), which formerly stood solitarily in an extensive landscape garden, built for the Russian ambassador Andrey Kirillovich Rasumofsky (Razumovsky), best known from the three string quartets (opus 59) by Beethoven dedicated to him. The palace was the venue for the premiere of Beethoven's Fifth Symphony and a social focal point. After a fire on New Year's Eve 1814/15 the garden wing had to be rebuilt. Inside however Montoyer's décor has been to a large extent preserved. Another garden palace is the Clam-Gallas palace, constructed in 1834/35 by Koch for Franz Josef Dietrichstein and unchanged in its location in the midst of a spacious park.

A major work of Viennese neo-Classicism is the equestrian statue of Joseph II from 1801–03 by the sculptor Zauner on the Josephsplatz before the Imperial Library. The reforming emperor is represented as a Roman general, in allusion to the statue of Marcus Aurelius on the Roman Capitol. The monument of Francis I in the Inneren Burghof courtyard of the Imperial palace was created in 1838–46 by Pompeo Marchesi from Milan.

Franz Anton Zauner, equestrian statue of Emperor Joseph II, Josephsplatz, 1795, realised in 1801–03

The Age of Emperor Francis Joseph (1848–1916)

History

Francis Joseph, the Habsburg emperor who reigned longest, enjoyed great popularity despite military and foreign policy failures. The ancient emperor was the symbol of an ancient monarchy and as such the only force that in the end held the multinational state together till its collapse in the First World War. Francis Joseph came to the throne as an 18-year old after his uncle's abdication. An almost successful assassination attempt by a Hungarian tailor on 18 February 1853 earned him sympathy among the people.

The courageous intervention of a citizen and the widespread wishes for recovery demonstrated how widely he was recognised as the representative of the monarchy. After military defeats to France and Sardinia (Magenta and Solferino 1859) and the loss of Lombardy however Francis Joseph was compelled to make political concessions in order to ensure the support of the upper middle class and thus prevent a national bankruptcy. The new local council in Vienna, soon a leading social institution, was formed in 1861. Further foreign policy disasters occurred with the defeat against the Prus-

The Kiss, Gustav Klimt, 1907–08, oil on canvas, Austrian Gallery Belvedere. The Kiss is one of Gustav Klimt's (1862–1918) – and Jugendstil's – most significant works

Josef Laugl, Vienna during the World Expo in 1873

sian army at Königgrätz on 3 July 1866, the subsequent loss of the Venetian province to Italy and the exclusion of Austria from the German unification process. As a consequence, the "Compromise" with Hungary in 1867 elevated it to an autonomous state under a common government (the double monarchy) and a liberal "December Constitution" was enacted, introducing a division of power and a guarantee of civil rights for the first time.

Under the autonomous and legally empowered local council a liberal economy grew at the cost of an impoverished working class rapidly expanding with the steady influx from the eastern regions of the empire (900,000 inhabitants in 1890 without the suburbs). Around 1880 about 65% of Vienna's population consisted of immigrants, in 1910 a half million people alone in the Viennese conurbation were of Czech descent. The positive results of this period of rapid economic growth, known as the Gründerzeit, were major civic projects such as the Central Cemetery (from 1873 on) and the long overdue regulation of the Danube after floods and ice jams (1870–75), as well as the fifth and till then the largest World Expo in 1873 in the Prater, with a main building which caused a sensation as the largest dome in the world (108m diameter). An urban railway was under construction since 1893 and a section inaugurated in 1898. While the improvement of the catastrophic living conditions in the slums only partially succeeded, the introduction of general and equal suffrage (for men) was achieved in 1907.

Emperor Francis Joseph I, painting by Franz Winterhalter, 1865, Sissi-Museum

Empress Elisabeth ("Sisi"), painting by Franz Winterhalter, 1865, Sissi-Museum

The last two decades before the collapse of the imperial monarchy are regarded as its most brilliant period, thanks to the intellectual and cultural riches of the city. In the legendary coffeehouses a self-contained world with its hierarchies and circles thrived, in which the writers Arthur Schnitzler, Hugo von Hofmannsthal, Stefan Zweig or Karl Kraus rose to fame. Not only literature was shaken by Sigmund Freud's "Interpretation of Dreams" (1899). Architects and visual artists abandoned the opulent Historicism of the Ring Boulevard and founded on 22 May 1897 the Secession artists group. A last great musical flourishing occurred with the lied cycles of Hugo Wolf, the reforms of Gustav Mahler (1897–1907 director of the Imperial Opera) and particularly the circle around Arnold Schönberg, whose works regularly sparked scandals during their premieres. Following the era of Johann Strauss senior and junior (died 1899) popular operetta celebrated new success with Fran Lehár.

Votive Church, Heinrich von Ferstel, 1856–79

Votive Church, Heinrich von Ferstel, 1856–79

The Ring Boulevard

In 1850 the old ring wall of bastions with the empty strips of land before it still existed. The eradication of this highly ana-

Todesco Palace (Kärntner Straße 51), Ludwig Förster and Theodor Hansen, 1861–64

chronistic remnant, unacceptable for a city approaching a million inhabitants, although repeatedly called for, was prevented above all by military reasons (during the revolution of 1848 the old ring wall had provided valuable protection against the proletarian masses from the suburbs). Finally in 1857 the emperor ordered that the Ring Boulevard be constructed. The precise ideas of Francis Joseph, and the integration of a last palace project, prove that he regarded the Ring Boulevard as a symbol of power. At the same time it offered the upper class the opportunity of displaying its recently acquired wealth and high standard of life in adequately prestigious architecture in the immediate vicinity of the high aristocracy. The immense project was financed by the sale of a fifth of the building land. While three fifths of the total 2.4 million sq. m. were devoted to streets, parks and squares, a further fifth was planned for public buildings. These magnificent buildings have been recognised as major works of the European architecture of Historicism.

Demolition of the bastions begun in spring 1858. Soon the City Park was created (opened 1862) with the Kursalon concert hall (Johann Garben, 1865–67). While the prestigious buildings are concentrated in the west near the Imperial palace (Burgring and Town Hall Quarter), the northern section (Schottenring) with the Stock Exchange was reserved for the financial aristocracy. Construction in this area had already begun before the actual creation of the Ring Boulevard with work on a major building, the Votive Church, a foundation to commemorate, and on the site of, the failed assassinati-

Edmund Hellmer, Memorial for Johann Strauß junior in City Park, from 1904, unveiled in 1921

on attempt on the emperor in 1853. The entire conception up to the appeal for donations in all parts of the empire and the lack of an apparent religious function (from 1878 University Church) reveals the clear and intended parallels to the building of St Charles in the early 18th century. Aside from its purpose as a monument-church to the emperor and to the unity of the monarchy, the Votive Church was also intended to serve as a temple of fame, as a burial monument for famous Austrians (cf. Westminster Abbey in London, Panthéon in Paris). However only the Renaissance tomb of Count Salm, the defender of Vienna in 1529, was placed in the church. In architectural and technical aspects this prestige project built in 1856–79 according to plans by Ferstel was innovative for Vienna, where such a

State Opera, former Imperial Opera, August Sicard von Sicardsburg and Eduard van der Nüll, 1861–69

Karl Kundmann, Schubert Memorial in City Park, 1872

Parliament (Dr.-Karl-Renner-Ring 3), Theophil Hansen, 1874–83

Fountain with statue of
Pallas Athena before the
Parliament, Karl Kund-
mann, 1898–1902

"stylistically pure" neo-Gothic was just as unusual as a realisation "appropriate to the materials used" in cut stone without plaster, following medieval craft traditions. That this choice of style and manner of construction for the planned national Austrian church was a political decision should be obvious, even if Ferstel adhered to the French High Gothic. The un-medieval raising of the edifice by means of a base plate fully qualifies it as a monument.

The Imperial Opera on the site of the former Kärntnertor gate was constructed in 1861–69 by the renowned architects Sicardsburg and van der Null, whose deaths (suicide and heart attack) as a result

of the harsh criticism they received belonged to the concomitants of an architectural issue controversially discussed in the broad public sphere. The façades and interior are full of imaginative allusions to the forms of art and themes from music theatre; galleries and arcaded passages lend the exterior a vigorous life of its own.

One of the first "Zinspalais" ("rental palaces") of Historicism with the traditional division into a commercial zone for shops on the ground floor, piano nobile for the property owners and rented flats in the upper stories is the palace for the bankers Eduard and Moritz von Todesco (1861–64) opposite the Opera. The luxu-

Town Hall, Friedrich von Schmidt, 1872–83, main façade

rious rooms in the piano nobile (ball and dining rooms) strikingly illustrate the pervasive imitation of the aristocratic lifestyle by upper class parvenus. The palace on the Kärntnerring constructed for Duke Philip of Württemberg in 1862–65 (already converted to a hotel in 1872/72) is a monumental example of severe Historicism in the forms of the New Viennese Renaissance.

Numerous memorials were raised in the City Park which originated not from imperial but from civic initiatives, honouring figures from outside the court and the military. The earliest of these memorials, erected in 1872 by the Viennese Men's Singing Association, displays

Schubert in a moment of composing. The culmination of these memorials is the ornate monument for Johann Strauss junior (since 1904, unveiled in 1921), portraying the composer as a gilded bronze figure under marble round arches with pairs of muses in relief.

In the 1870s huge prominent buildings for various institutions were erected. The Town Hall, constructed in 1872–83 according to plans by Friedrich von Schmidt from the Cologne stonemason's lodge, is the quintessential monument of civic self-representation. The dimensions and even more the sensational appearance of the radically neo-Gothic building overshadow all the other buildings in the

Burgtheater (Dr.-Karl-Lueger-Ring 2), Gottfried Semper and Karl von Hasenauer, 1874–88

bottom left: Stock Exchange (Schottenring 16), Theophil Hansen, 1873–77

bottom right: Musikverein [Concert Hall] (Dumbastraße 3), Theophil Hansen, 1867–70

vicinity. The robust tower recalls Flemish town halls from the 15th century, the vast staircase and banqueting hall suggest a powerful municipal government with forms derived from the late Gothic architecture of the Hanseatic league. When one considers the historical situation, the political and commercial insignificance of the Viennese citizenry precisely in the period imitated here, then the typical discrepancy of the Gründerzeit between emblematic aspirations and actual reality becomes manifest.

The venerable university likewise received a new building (in Renaissance style) on the Paradestraße. The interior rooms and courtyards quote Italian palaces (inner courtyard Palazzo Farnese) and university buildings studied there previously by the architect Ferstel.

The Parliament was erected by Hansen in 1874–83 in a programmatic neo-Greek style (birth of democracy in Greece). At the same time he built the Stock Exchange on the Schottenring as a neo-Re-

naissance edifice. While the Stock Exchange employs the basilica type, developed for other such buildings with this function (Hamburg Stock Exchange 1837–41), the Parliament in its formal language and disposition of space is related to the Capitol in Washington (1850–63). The array of sculptures on the façade and especially in the meeting rooms is exceptionally lavish. The Ring Boulevard period was also an epoch of buildings for public performances. Aside from the Opera, the increasing speciali-

sation of performing disciplines led to buildings for concerts and dramatic theatre. In 1867–70 Hansen constructed the Musikverein am Karlsplatz, the first pure concert hall in Vienna, equipped with a large auditorium and a chamber music hall. A completely different character is displayed by the Hofburgtheater built in 1874–88 by Semper and Hasenauer as part of the expansion planned for the Imperial Palace. The monumental late Historicism theatre draws on forms from the High Renaissance and from Baroque décor. The focal point of the Ring Boulevard is the Imperial Forum with the Neue Burg [New Castle], integrating the museums of Fine Arts and of Natural History. After a long planning phase Vienna was able to engage Semper, at that time the most celebrated architect in Europe, whose conceptually and dimensionally unique expansion plans of 1869 were initiated but could not be completed due to the outbreak of the First World War. Semper collaborated with Hasenauer, who after the

Imperial Palace, Neue Burg, Gottfried Semper and Karl von Hasenauer, 1879–1923

University (Dr.-Karl-Lueger-Ring 1), Heinrich Ferstel, 1873–84, main façade

Maria Theresa Memorial in front of the Museum of Fine Arts, bronze statues by Caspar Zumbusch, 1888

Museum of Fine Arts, east interior courtyard with sgraffiti (personifications of arts and trades), Ferdinand Laufberger

death of the great architect in 1879 constructed the South Wing of the "Neue Burg" (North Wing never built).

Museum Buildings

The buildings of the Museums of Fine Art and of Natural History erected in 1871–91 according to plans by Semper and Hasenauer belong to the most significant museum buildings in the world. They have earned this status by the expressive combination of imperial ideology in the design of the monumental square with the most modern architectural language and up-to-date demands on a public museum. Nowhere else is the presentation of princely patronage and collecting as justified as here, since the Habsburg collections vividly demonstrate an almost unbroken tradition reaching back to the late Middle Ages. Semper's plans prevailed above all because of the expansive design of the square, with the Imperial Forum extending beyond the Ring Boulevard and the symmetrically positioned, free-standing museums prolonging the

wings of the New Burg. The long two-storey buildings with two inner courtyards each were subordinated to the square, concealing their immense horizontal dimensions by shifting the octagonal dome, normally over the staircase in the building's centre, to the façades. The uniformly high-quality sculptures, created by sculptors such as Johannes Benk, Karl Kundmann and Hellmer, are convincingly arranged. Noteworthy are the allegories of painting and sculpture flanking the main entrance and on the attic balustrade the statues of artists from Apelles to Moritz von Schwind.

Just as significant is the interior décor by Hasenauer, who after Semper's volunta-

Natural History Museum, Gottfried Semper and Karl von Hasenauer, 1871–91, façade towards Imperial Forum (Maria-Theresia-Platz)

Museum of Fine Arts, Gottfried Semper and Karl von Hasenauer, 1871–91, façade to Imperial Forum, in front Maria Theresa Memorial, Alfred von Arneth (conception), Caspar von Zumbusch (design), Carl von Hasenauer (plinth architecture), 1874–88

Raffael, Madonna in the Country, 1505/06, Museum of Fine Arts

Vermeer, The Art of Painting, circa 1670, Museum of Fine Arts

above right: ceiling painting in the Great Staircase, Apotheosis of Art der Kunst, Michael Munkásy, 1889/90

Austrian Museum for Applied Arts, former Imperial Austrian Museum for Art and Industry (Stubenring 3–5), Heinrich Ferstel, 1866–71

ry departure in 1876 due to persistent conflicts over the direction of construction. Here too the leading contemporary Viennese painters were engaged, including Hans Makart, Franz von Matsch and Hans Caron, as well as Ernst and Gustav Klimt. The ceiling of the exceptionally lavish staircase is adorned with an Apotheosis of Art by the Hungarian painter Munkásy. Via this staircase, on whose half-landing the famous Theseus group by Canova is displayed, the visitor reaches the highpoint, the Pantheon-like dome with the portrait medallions of the Habsburg patrons. The upper ground floor contains Egyptian and classical antiquities, the weapons collecti-

on and applied arts, the second floor the heart of the museum, the gallery of paintings.

Aside from these two major museums for the imperial and royal collections further buildings were raised during the formation of the Ring Boulevard for the extensive collections of diverse institutions. The Austrian Museum of Art and Industry, built by Ferstel in 1866–71, was the second applied arts museum in the world after the Victoria & Albert Museum in London. The building for the institution, founded shortly before in 1863 by the emperor, was at the same time the first museum building on the Ring Boulevard. In its succession of rooms (vestibule, interior courtyard, staircase) it adheres to Italian palaces. Ferstel also designed the Applied Arts School (now the University for Applied Arts) erected in 1875–77, institutionally linked to the museum and adjoining it to the north. Today the museum, known as the Museum for Applied Arts (MAK) and modernised in 1986-93, belongs to the outstanding cultural venues in the city with its excellent collections and temporary exhibits.

The long-standing institution of the Academy for Visual Arts received a building on the Operring, built in 1872–75 following plans by Hansen and clearly set back from the magnificent boulevard. The four-storey, castle-like edifice surprises the visitor with an interesting use of colour in the façade's design. The only partially exhibited, extensive collection of paintings, drawings and prints is of great importance, originating for the most part in gifts from the 19th centu-

ry and thus documenting the patronage of the Viennese aristocracy and upper class.

The only 30-year-old Olbrich, an employee of the leading representative of modern architecture in Vienna, Otto Wagner, erected at Karlsplatz the world-famous exhibition building for the Association of Visual Artists of Austria, the Viennese Secession. The Secession was founded by the separation of a group of artists from the increasingly conservative and anti-innovative Association of Visual Artists of Austria founded in 1861, following the example of the Munich Secession formed in 1892. Financing of construction came from the abundant proceeds of the 1st Exhibition of the Secession (in the rooms of the Garden

Building Society on the Ring Boulevard) and from private art patrons such as Karl Wittgenstein. The building's architecture, influenced by a design from the president of the artists' association Gustav Klimt, differs drastically from the Academy building only a few years older as

above and bottom: Secession Exhibition Hall (Friedrichstraße 12), Joseph Maria Olbricht, 1897/98

Carl von Zamboni, In Café Griensteidl, photo for "Die vornehme Welt", before 1897

Café Griensteidl, 1847, view from Michaelerplatz, photo before 1897

Herberstein Palace (Café Griensteidl), 1897, view from Michaelerplatz

well as from usual museum architecture. The functional, indulgingly fragmented Academy building by the representative of Historicism Hansen exhibits the strongest conceivable contrast to the exceedingly pathetic "art temple" by Olbrich. The façade with the programmatic inscription "Der Zeit ihre Kunst. Der Kunst ihre Freiheit" [To the age its art. To art its freedom] is the embodiment of symbolist architecture: Un-ornamented blocks flank the set-back entrance, marked by the gilded friezes of foliage and three female busts (symbols of painting, sculpture and architecture) which seem to announce an Egyptian temple. The building is crowned by a three-fourths dome, a gigantic sphere made of a mesh of gilded iron laurel leaves, an explosive – as regards art policies – allusion to Apollo, leader of the muses and patron of the arts. The open and floating qualities of the construction create a symbolic connection between heaven and earth, underlining the religious connotations. The central hall however is purely functional and was meant to be transformed for each exhibition. For the 14th Exhibition of the Secession in 1902 for example the interior was focussed completely on the main display, Klinger's Beethoven statue, accompanied by Klimt's Beethoven frieze, today displayed in the cellar.

The Viennese Coffeehouse

Many of Vienna's coffeehouses are world-famous and have often been copied, none however has survived in its original form since their heyday around 1900. Innumerable legends and anecdotes, scholarly investigations and psychological studies have made them well-known. They lived from their guests, their circles, their unwritten rules at the tables.

The first legendary coffeehouse was the Griensteidl, located where the Schauflergasse ended at Michaelerplatz. The café opened in 1847 by the pharmacist Heinrich Griensteidl became the central meeting point around 1890 of the "Young Viennese" writers centred around Hermann Bahr (publisher of the weekly "Die Zeit"), including Peter Altenberg, Hugo von Hofmannsthal, Arthur Schnitzler, Felix Salten and initially Karl Kraus. When the coffeehouse was demolished in 1897 the regular customers celebrated the demise of the establishment with a magnificent funeral meal, as Kraus recorded in his satiric memorandum (Die demolirte Litteratur [Demolished Literature]). In its place the Herberstein Palace in the over-or-

nate late style of the Ring Boulevard was erected (in 1990 a new Café Griensteidl was opened on the ground floor). The Michaelerplatz, rich in tradition, was now to become more urbane; the Drei-lauferhaus (1799) extending far into the square also hindered such ambitions. In its place a new building was erected for the tailoring firm of Goldman & Salatsch in 1909–11, one of the outstanding works of Viennese Jugendstil. Adolf Loos adhered to the requirements of be-velling the corner and orienting the main façade towards the square, but his radically unadorned façade incited one of the building scandals so typical of Vienna. The effects of the stark contrast between the noble building material (Euboean marble) of the lower, promi-nent storeys and the naked wall of the residential storeys above corresponds to the functional division of the building, and thus to modern demands that archi-tectural form had to follow function. Loos was, it can be added, the leading coffeehouse architect of his time. His Café Museum (1899) was predestined for fame thanks to its proximity to the Academy of Visual Arts, the Secession exhibition hall and Technical College. Here writers (Kraus, Werfel, Musil, Ca-netti, Roth), musicians (Lehár, Alban Berg) and artists (Klimt, Schiele, Ko-koschka, Trakl) convened. Loos not on-ly designed the façade, but also the en-tire interior décor with wall coverings, display cabinets, furniture and billiard tables (reconstructed 2003), for which conspicuously luxurious materials (ma-hogany, polished brass) were employed. Loos likewise provided a total design for the American Bar (1908), a sensation of

the period. After the closing of the Griensteidl the Young Viennese moved to the nearby Café Central, opened in the former main hall of the Austrian-Hungarian National Bank in 1868. The

Loos House, former Goldman & Salatsch Building (Michaeler-platz 3), Adolf Loos, 1909-11

Ferstel Palace, former Austrian-Hungarian National Bank and Café Central (Herren-gasse 14), Heinrich von Ferstel, 1856–60

Kärntnerbar, original-
ly American Bar
(Kärntner Straße 10,
Kärntner Durchgang),
Adolf Loos, 1908,
façade renovated

Rossauer Barracks
(9th district), Karl Pil-
hal and Karl Markl,
1865–69

establishment has been frequently described and quickly became famous, Ferstel's neo-Renaissance style and the unusual height for a coffeehouse of the former bank hall continue to define its character today.

Functional Architecture

The fighting during the 1848 revolution had exposed the strategic importance of the old bastions. In order to be able to bombard the city from higher
ground and at the same time to serve as
a bulwark against proletarian masses flowing in from the suburbs, military bases
were set up outside of the outer line of
fortifications (the Linienwall) before the
construction of the Ring Boulevard. On
slightly higher terrain southeast of the city centre the Arsenal was constructed
from 1849 on, a gigantic complex in
rectangular shape with sides up to 700m
long. The entire armaments industry of

the period was concentrated here, together with a Weapons Museum, initially
planned as an armoury and the first true
museum building in Vienna, a hospital,
a church and a warehouse. Most of the
buildings were built by Sicardsburg and
van der Null, including the commander's
building, which serves as the main entrance from the city. It presents itself as
a richly adorned edifice of undisguised
brick with cut stone ornaments, the somewhat Gothic forms recall Romantic
castle architecture, the large niche sculptures symbolise the theory and practice
of the Austrian arts of war. The architectural highpoint of the immense barracks
complex is the Weapons Museum, whose broad front appears directly behind
the entrance gate. For the façade Hansen resorted to Oriental motifs, the central projection crowned by a dome resembles an Ottoman tomb building, the
trios of windows and œil-de-bœufs as
well as the decorative window tracery
all stem from the Islamic-Byzantine

world. For the wall surfaces Hansen employed variously coloured bricks and thus created the impression of a Gothic citadel. Other barracks were constructed in response to the revolutionary fighting in 1848 to form a triangle of fortifications with the Arsenal: the Franz Josephs Barracks on the Stubenring (demolished in 1898) and the Rudolf Barracks (today Rossauer Barracks). The latter, constructed by Colonel Pilhat and Major Markl in 1865–69, is also a neo-Gothic fortification of undisguised brick with a stepped façade and battlements. It is considerably smaller (270m long) and less ornamental in its details as the Arsenal, yet its dynamic front of many setbacks and projections has an excellent effect in the urban context (main façade towards the Danube canal). The most importantly oriented towards the courtyard.

A major work of European industrial architecture is the Simmering gasometer. The largest gasworks in Europe at the time, located on the Danube canal southeast of the city, was formed in 1896–99 by the fusion of various smaller suppliers. The international competition was won by the Berlin engineer Schimming, whose design was realised with modifications by Kapaun from the municipal building office. The dome-shaped, suspended roofs in iron construction made of open hearth iron and wood lagging represent a technical masterpiece. The four gas tanks were transformed into flats and shopping facilities following highly-regarded plans by Coop Himmelblau, Jean Nouvel, Wilhelm Holzbauer and Manfred Wehdorn.

The competition for a design for a church at the Am Steinhof mental hospital to the west of Vienna was won in 1904 by Otto Wagner, the most famous Viennese architect of his time. Following his plans the entire complex was constructed in 1904–07 in the pavilion system, with an adjoining Pulmonology Centre to the west, formerly for wealthy mentally ill patients. The architectural design and décor (sculptures by von

above: Arsenal (3d district), on the left Commander Building, August Sicard von Sicardsburg and Eduard van der Nüll, 1849–56, Main façade with niche figures by Hans Gasser: in the middle Austria (1853), left Caster, Armourer, Wainwright and Fitter, right Mathematics, Physics, Mechanics and Chemistry (1858)

below: Arsenal, Military Museum (former Weapons Museum), Theophil Hansen, 1852–56, figures by Hans Gasser: below Bravery, Loyalty, Sacrifice and Martial Intelligence, above Strength, Justice, Religion and History (1854)

Simmering Gasometer (11th district), Franz Kapaun, 1896–99

Villa Wagner I (Hüttelbergstraße 26, 14th district), Otto Wagner, 1886–88

Villa Wagner II (Hüttelbergstraße 28, 14th district), Otto Wagner, 1912/13

Franz von Matsch (design), Franz Siegel (copper repoussé) and Andrea Francini (stonemasonry), Ankeruhr [Anchor Clock] on bridge between Ankerhof and adjacent building (Hoher Markt 10–11), 1911–17, in the middle figure of Prince Eugene

Schimkowitz and Carl Ederer, mosaics by Remigius Geyler, glass painting by Moser) are of the highest quality and adhere at the same time to the demands of strict functionality. This applies to the friendly appearance of the bright interior, which follows explicit therapeutic objectives, and the optimistic content of the images, as well as the avoidance of dangerous edges in the church, the washable tile floor, heating, facilities for air circulation and flowing water in the stoup.

A comprehensive total conception likewise forms the basis for the two villas which Wagner built for himself, also on the western edge of the city in Hütteldorf. Their construction is separated by a quarter of a century, making them an instructive example of the stylistic evolution of this leading Viennese Jugendstil architect. The first Summer House (1886–88) corresponds to the architectonic ideals of neo-Palladianism and in its setting in the surrounding nature to the aesthetic principles of the time. The house is dominated by the gallery in the middle section in Ionic order and the forward projecting roof – a typical Wagner motif. The architect sold the house built for his family after his children had grown up, and erected in 1912/13 a smaller house on an adjacent property. The first villa was purchased in 1972 by Ernst Fuchs, a painter of Fantastic Realism, reformed and opened to the public as a private museum in 1988. The second villa designed in 1905 is in contrast to the first one an extremely plain and asymmetrical building, whose décor is limited to the window zone in the

Am Steinhof Church, Otto Wagner, 1905–07, façade and interior

Am Steinhof Church, Koloman Moser, glass window in left transept: The Seven Works of Charity, 1905–07

Central Cemetery, Dr. Karl Lueger Memorial Church, Max Hegele and Ludwig Zatzka, 1908–10, view for the east

ground floor and the door frame with a glass mosaic above (Leopold Forstner following a design by Moser).

The construction of the urban railway, since 1894 under the artistic direction of Wagner, represented one of the largest projects at the turn of the century. Numerous stations, technical facilities and routes (U4 and U6 lines) have been

preserved unchanged. Due to a regulation preventing the railways from running at the same grade with streets, the routes are characterised by viaducts on undisguised brick arches, bridges and tunnels. The stations, particularly Schönbrunn, Kettenbrückengasse and Karlsplatz on the U4, number among the most famous in Europe together with those of the urban railways in Paris and Berlin. The Viennese stations were planned up to the last detail by Wagner, following his conception of a functional architecture as well as the demands for the appropriate use of materials and for technical clarity. An incunabulum of modern architecture is Wagner's Postsparkasse (Post Savings Bank, 1904–12). Strictly speaking it belongs to the Ring Boulevard, from which it is separated by Georg-Coch-Platz. Individual structural elements of the main front such as the emphasis on the central projection or the crowning genii made of aluminium, symbolising the spirits of transport and thriftiness (Othmar Schimkowitz), recall Historicist façade designs. The renouncement of any ornament not structurally necessary and the deliberate display of the aluminium bolts used to hold the granite and marble panels however constitute a declaration for radical functionality. This is all the more true for the design of the interior, the bright offices, the meeting rooms and particularly the huge central bank hall, which makes do without any type of traditional architectural ennoblement and is completely defined by the materials glass, iron and aluminium. This aesthetic of materials, which conspicuously exposed the futuristic warm air ducts till

Pavilions at Karlsplatz, Otto Wagner, circa 1898

then always concealed, proved highly seminal.

Jugendstil décor visibly shapes Vienna's urban image. The architectural examples of Wagner and Loos, the demanding criteria of the Wiener Werkstätten as well as the pre-existing structure of high-quality Baroque palaces helped Jugendstil décor to achieve a unique standard, unmistakeably defining the city's reputation. A last example is the so-called Ankeruhr [Anchor Clock], a picture clock with an organ mechanism adorning a bridge between the Ankerhof and an adjacent building at the Hoher Markt. The building was erected in 1912/14 by Ernst

von Gotthilf and Alexander Neumann, the clock in 1911–17 following a design by Matsch.

Imperial Pavilion of Urban Railway at Schönbrunn (13th district), Otto Wagner, 1898

Vienna after 1918

History

The political, social and cultural consequences of the First World War were more catastrophic in Vienna than in any other European metropolis. The 2.2 million city (1914), fifth largest in the world, was suddenly an over-dimensioned capital at the edge of a small state. The abdication of the last emperor Charles, who on 11 November 1918 forwent "every participation in state affairs", was at the same time the abdication of an entire epoch with its self-conception, an epoch which had brought forth countless writers and artists. The description of a vanished age provided quite a few writers with their literary leitmotiv, even when they left Vienna, such as Stefan Zweig (Salzburg) and Joseph Roth (Berlin, Paris).

The years after the collapse were marked by political tensions previously unknown in Austria. The First Republic initially consisted of a coalition of social democrats and Christian socialists: in April 1920 it broke apart. In Vienna a social-democratic government ruled from 1919; it succeeded in separating the city from Lower Austria (effective on 1 January 1922) and subsequently realised unique building projects to solve the tremendous lack of living space. "Red Vienna" came to an end in 1934 due to a renewed failure of the large coalition at the federal level, to the loss in the traumatic civil war in February and to the victory of the conservatives. On 13 March 1938 Hitler made his entrance into the ci-

ty, which during an aerial bombardment in March 1945 suffered its heaviest destruction since 1683. The period after 1945 was initially dominated by reconstruction. Thanks to events in 1989 with the opening of the borders between eastern and western Europe, as well as the ensuing entry into the EU of the neighbouring eastern countries, Vienna recovered the leading position in eastern Central Europe it had enjoyed before 1945.

Red Vienna: Buildings of the First Republic

The social-democratic government developed a model of a new city, which in contrast to the dominant situation before 1918 followed the ideals of social justice and equality among people. Tax increases to finance the major residential building projects to relieve the impoverished masses lacking employment and

p. 116: Hundertwasser House (Löwengasse 41–43, 3d district), Friedensreich Hundertwasser, 1985–90

Crematorium (11th district), Clemens Holzmeister, 1921–23

Amalie Baths (Reumannplatz 23, 10th district), Otto Nadel and Karl Schmalhofer, 1923–26

Reumannhof (Margaretengürtel 100–110, 5th district), Hubert Gessner, 1924

living space fell overwhelmingly on the wealthy. Immense blocks of flats were raised, some with an almost fortified character; their quality of life was much higher than in the tenements from the late 19th century. In addition great store was set on common facilities such as nursery schools, sports halls and open spaces, just as much as on public services buildings like hospitals, schools and employment offices. By 1934 approximately 65,000 new flats had been erected.

A major work of expressionist architecture in Austria is the Crematorium, constructed in 1921–23 according to plans by Holzmeister on the grounds of the Renaissance palace of Neugebäude opposite the Central Cemetery. The Amalia Baths of 1923–26 (so named after the social-democratic councillor Amalie Pölzer) is one of the most important buildings of Red Vienna, as well as an architectural expression of the new form of government. The largest indoor swimming pool in Europe at that time has numerous additional pools and is decorated inside in a highly modern style, including a moveable glass roof. The best-known of the major residential building projects of Red Vienna is the Karl-Marx-Hof (1926–33); as the "worker's fortress" it was the site of fighting during the civil war in February 1934 and the target of national-socialist attacks. The gigantic, more than 1 km long complex (super-block), the third largest of its kind in Vienna, with over 1300 flats, shops, offices, a nursery school and a library, is the materialised ideal of communal living of the social-democratic government. The fronts towards the street and the courtyard are three-dimensionally formed and correspondingly differentiated by their colour from the double-shell superstructure. Other inner city residential blocks are also important as regards urban planning. The Reumannhof (1924) for example, named after Vienna's first social-democratic mayor, was the earliest of the large Viennese residential complexes with a building front towards the street enclosing an inner courtyard. Its imposing eight-storey central block (originally 16 storeys planned) sets a dominant signal on the "Ring Boulevard of the Proletariat", an accurate description of the Margaretengürtel even today. As an alternative to the inner city perimeter development, sizeable settlements were built at the city's edge with broad areas of green and varied residential housing. The largest of this kind, and at the same time the most extensive Viennese residential complex of the First Republic, was the Sandleitnerhof (1924–28) in the former sand pits in Ottakring. Here a

Karl-Marx-Hof (Heiligenstädter Straße 82–92, 19th district), Karl Ehn, 1926–33, cour d'honneur front

much broader variety of residential housing types and structures dominate, with park-like areas and intimate squa-

Sandleitnerhof (Sandleitengasse, 16th district), Emil Hoppe et. al, 1924–28

res. The Karl-Seitz-Hof (1926–31) in Floridsdorf on the other side of the Danube is regarded as a "workers' palace"; its monumental main building is arranged around the half-circle of a square (today a park) originally planned with a memorial. The last "superblock" and the second largest residential building of Red Vienna is the Engelsplatzhof in Brigittenau, erected in 1930–33 by Rudolf Perco, a leading disciple of Wagner, on a prominent site at the Florisdorfer Bridge. The design of the square as a cour d'honneur with flanking flagpoles is extremely distinctive, the abstaining from plastic details reinforces the monumental impression. The Viennese Werkbundsiedlung [Work Federation Settlement] (1930–32), the last of its kind in

Karl Marx Hof, Joseph Riedl, majolica figure of Charity

city by 31 architects (among them Holzmeister, Loos and Neutra from Vienna as well as Gerrit Rietveld, Hugo Häring and André Lurçat). Of the numerous buildings the rounded, by means of cylinder-like staircases vertically structured, row houses by Lurçat (Veitingergasse 87–93) are probably the most striking.

Engelsplatzhof (Friedrich-Engels-Platz, 20th district), Rudolf Perco, 1930–33

Europe, was a lately realised alternative to the residential building programme of Red Vienna. A total of 70 "houses with flats of the smallest kind" were erected on a property in Lainz southwest of the

Visual Art from 1918 till today

In 1918 almost the entire Viennese art scene collapsed. The departure or death of the outstanding painters and foremost sculptors created a vacuum that the next generation could hardly fill. Vienna surrendered its status as a leading international art centre. One of the most significant sculptors after 1918 was Anton Hanak, who discarded his Secessionist past and discovered a new sense of physicalness approaching New Objectivism. His marble Magna Mater fountain (circa 1925) with a female figure surrounded by children illustrates this, just as much as his portrait bust of Victor Adler for the Republic monument, raised in 1928 on occasion of the tenth anniversary of the founding of the Republic.

As teachers at the Academy the painters Herbert Boeckl and Albert Paris Gütersloh, together with Hanak's pupil the sculptor Fritz Wotruba, were the most important lodestars of the wave of renovation that set in after 1945. Aside from Wotruba's major sculptures in the Museum for the 20th Century, his principal work is the Church of the Most Holy Tri-

Werkbund Settlement (13th district), Veitingergasse 87, André Lurçat, 1932

Visual Art from 1918 till today

Anton Hanak, Magna Mater Fountain, circa 1925, originally in the Lustkandlgasse 50 (9th district), installed in 1965 in Liesinger Rathauspark (Speisinger Straße 223, 23d district)

nity on the site of a former anti-aircraft barracks on the Georgenberg, designed by him and built in 1974–76.

One of his many important disciples is Alfred Hrdlicka. Aside from portraits his vast oeuvre includes several political monuments, such as his controversial Memorial against War and Fascism (1991) made of Carrara marble on the Albertinaplatz.

Painting in the 1960s and 1970s was likewise renewed completely. Especially famous at that time were the representatives of the Viennese school of Fantastic Realism. The representationalism of their pictures was, like the sculptures of the closely associated Hrdlicka, directed against abstract art, but also against the spectacular performances of the Viennese Actionists of the 1960s. They developed a surrealistic visual language with exceptional draughtsmanship,

drawing on mythological and Christian themes and a manner of painting derived from the Old Masters. Major figures included Ernst Fuchs, Anton Lehm-

above left: Republic Memorial (corner Schmerlingplatz/Dr.-Karl-Renner-Ring) with bronze busts of social-democratic politicians of the first Republic: Jakob Reumann (by Franz Seifert), Victor Adler (Anton Hanak) and Ferdinand Hanusch (Carl Wollek, copy by Mario Petrucci, 1948), erected 1928, removed 1934 and re-installed 1948

above centre: Ernst Fuchs, sculptures in garden of Villa Wagner I (Hüttelbergstraße 26, 14th district), after 1972

Alfred Hrdlicka, Memorial against War and Fascism, Albertinaplatz, 1991

Westbahnhof, train station (Europaplatz 1, 15th district), Robert Hartinger, Joseph Wöhnhart and Franz Xaver Schlarbaum, 1949–51

right: Central Savings Bank (Favoritenstraße 118, 10th district), Günther Domenig, 1975–79

den and above all Rudolf Hausner, whose excessively self-analytical paintings (the so-called Adam series) number among the most remarkable works of recent Viennese painting. Fuchs purchased the first villa by Wagner in 1972 and reformed it into his private museum (opened in 1988); his notable sculptures and paintings decorate the gardens, façades and rooms. The most important representatives of abstract painting are Max Weiler, Markus Prachensky and Josef Mikl.

Stadthalle, exhibition hall (Vogelweidplatz, 15th district), Roland Rainer, 1953–58

Architecture after 1945

Air raids in the last days of the Second World War took the lives of 11,000 people and had devastating – although not on the scale of Hamburg, Frankfurt or Dresden – consequences for the historical material and infrastructure of Vienna, of which a third was destroyed. The symbols of reconstruction included the restoration of landmarks (St Stephen's Cathedral, Burgtheatre, Opera), bridges and streets, as well as the restructuring of the city, after 1950 with prominent new buildings. The Westbahnhof train station, built in 1949–51 on the site of the destroyed Kaiserin Elisabeth Bahnhof from 1858, represents in its ticketing hall facing the city the new beginning. It will relinquish its key role in international train transport however to the planned Central Train Station (2012). In contrast, the historical

District Heating Plant at Spittelau (9th district), painted as a pseudo-mosque in 1990 by Hundertwasser

Südbahnhof train station survived the war with hardly any damage, yet the general mood of beginning a new era led to its demolition and a new station (1955–61), which however will itself make way in 2010 to a new planned through station.

The Stadthalle exhibition centre (1953–58) north of the Westbahnhof has evolved into an architectural icon, as the first of these celebrated buildings by Roland Rainer (Bremen, Ludwigshafen). A controversial unique edifice is the former Zentralsparkasse [Central Savings Bank], erected in 1975–79 by Günther Domenig, a renowned member of the Graz School, in an architecturally mediocre part of the Favoritenstraße. The reinforced concrete building with a curtain wall of stainless steel plates is conceived as a foreign body that forces itself into the vacant lot and organically billows out. Its ex-

Hundertwasser House
(Löwengasse 41–43,
3d district), Friedens-
reich Hundertwasser,
1982–85

erected in 1982 according to his notions on a property provided by the municipal government (the first of the numerous Hundertwasser houses existing today). Interesting ideas include for example the planting of trees (tree tenants) on terraces and projections, whose growth requires continuous care by the other tenants, or the "window right" allowing the individual modification of the exterior wall to an arm's length around the window by the tenants, vividly questioning the relationship between inside and outside. After the KunstHausWien, a former furniture factory rebuilt by Hundertwasser in 1991 into his personal museum, the alteration of the heating plant at Spittelau in 1990 represents his most spectacular Viennese project. While the House in the Löwengasse truly raises doubts about the seriousness of Hundertwasser's credo, the urban planning requirements on the heating plant seem to have been fulfilled, as the enhancement of the passage from the University of Economics to the train station Spittelau shows.

terior skin appears wrinkled and visitors seem to be swallowed up by a wide-open mouth.

Extraordinary popularity has been reaped by the buildings of the painter and Actionist Hundertwasser. His blatant articulation of the principles of ecological architecture though have not earned him a very flattering reputation in architectural circles, as his so-called Hundertwasser Haus exemplifies, which he

Hans Hollein in contrast enjoys international fame. His new Haas Haus at Stephansplatz (1985–90) has sparked public protests. Hollein filled in a sensitive gap in the urban texture caused by the war by setting a strong accent opposite the dominating cathedral, accepting however its pre-eminence and establishing a relationship with its religious architecture via the motif of the cylinder-like bay window with roof-top sail. A more recent highpoint of Hollein's architecture in Vienna is the award-winning Media Tower for Generali Versicherung at the Donaukanal (2000). Aside from Hollein, the other key protagonists of the young Viennese architectural scene are Gustav Peichl and the office of Coop Himmelblau (Wolf Prix and Helmut Swiczinsky). As a functionalist, Peichl is indebted to Wagner. A homage to the Secession can be read in the portal of the art forum of the Österreichische Länderbank on the Freyung square. His apartment house on Wagramer Straße on the Donauinsel (1994) is a plain, blue and white cylinder (nicknamed "Obelix"). Immediately adjacent to it Coop Himmelblau have erected a contrasting, sophisticated high-rise with state-of-the-art technology (climate façade etc.).

Lastly, two major projects of the last few years that vividly demonstrate the Viennese principle of integrating the old in the new. The Main Library by Ernst Mayr (1999) lies in the Neubaugürtel at a distinctive interface between the inner city and the outer areas and over an underground railway route by Otto Wagner. The long building (150m) not only follows the course of the tracks, but also ingeniously integrates the historic underground station Burggasse, by making

Media Tower (Taborstraße 1–3, 2nd district), Hans Hollein, 2000

New Haas House at Stephansplatz, Hans Hollein, 1985–90

the library's main hall at the same time the entrance to the station. The second project is the alteration of the Museumsquartier on the grounds of the Baroque stables by Fischer von Erlach, one of the largest cultural complexes in the world. The square is dominated by the contrast of the white Muschelkalk façade of the Museum Leopold with the dark grey basalt lava of the MUMOK. Particularly positive is the opening of

Residential Tower in the Wagramer Straße (Kratochwjlestraße 12, 22nd district), Coop Himmelblau, 1994

right: Residential Tower in the Wagramer Straße (22nd district), Gustav Peichl, 1994

Main Library (Urban-Loritz-Platz 2a, 7th district), Ernst Mayr, 1999

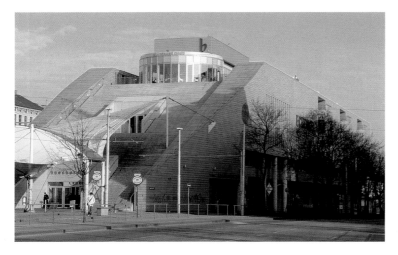

the pre-existing passageways in the Fischer building and thus the creation of an open square which can be ordinarily traversed, as well as the open spaces between the buildings with rest facilities. Today the MQ (Museumsquartier) is one of the most lively squares in the city and thanks to the modern orientation of the museums protected from mass tourism and Mozart-commercialism.

above: Museumsquartier (Museumsplatz 1, 7th district), Museum Moderner Kunst Stiftung Ludwig Wien (MUMOK), Ortner & Ortner, 1998–2001

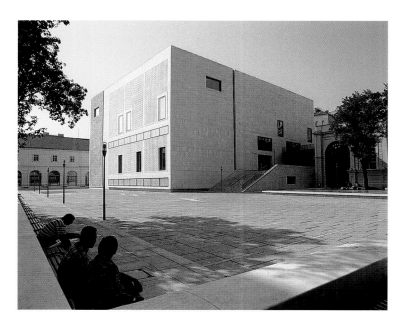

Museumsquartier, Leopold Museum, Ortner & Ortner, 1998–2001

Index

Photograph credits:
all photographs by Michael Imhof, Tobias Kunz and Michael Imhof Verlag GmbH & Co. KG
with the exception of:
Huberta Weigl, Vienna: p. 5, 15 bottom, 48 bottom, 49 above, 51, 72 above, 76, 93 bottom; 109 above, 125 bottom
wikipedia, p. 6 bottom, 30 bottom, 87, 96, 106 above, 111 above right;
akg-images, Berlin: p. 34 bottom, 53 above, 58, 63, 71, 94
IMAGNO/Austrian Archives, Vienna: p. 60/61
The Bridgeman Art Library, Berlin: p. 36 bottom
Collection of the Princes of Liechtenstein, Vaduz–Vienna: p. 67

© 2008
Michael Imhof Verlag GmbH & Co. KG
Stettiner Straße 25
D-36100 Petersberg
Tel. 0049/6 61/9 62 82 86
Fax 0049/6 61/6 36 86

Distribution in Austria:
Ennsthaler Gesellschaft mbH & Co. KG Stadtplatz 26, A-4400 Steyr
Tel. 07252 52053-20; Fax 07252 52053-22

Text: Tobias Kunz
Translation: David Sanchez, Madrid
Photos: Michael Imhof, Tobias Kunz and Huberta Weigl
Layout and Reproduction:
Michael Imhof Verlag
Printing and binding: Druckerei Uhl GmbH Co. KG, Radolfzell am Bodensee

Printed in EU

ISBN 978-3-86568-361-8